SpringerBriefs in Philosophy

SpringerBriefs present concise summaries of cutting-edge research and practical applications across a wide spectrum of fields. Featuring compact volumes of 50 to 125 pages, the series covers a range of content from professional to academic. Typical topics might include:

- A timely report of state-of-the art analytical techniques
- A bridge between new research results, as published in journal articles, and a contextual literature review
- A snapshot of a hot or emerging topic
- An in-depth case study or clinical example
- A presentation of core concepts that students must understand in order to make independent contributions

SpringerBriefs in Philosophy cover a broad range of philosophical fields including: Philosophy of Science, Logic, Non-Western Thinking and Western Philosophy. We also consider biographies, full or partial, of key thinkers and pioneers.

SpringerBriefs are characterized by fast, global electronic dissemination, standard publishing contracts, standardized manuscript preparation and formatting guidelines, and expedited production schedules. Both solicited and unsolicited manuscripts are considered for publication in the SpringerBriefs in Philosophy series. Potential authors are warmly invited to complete and submit the Briefs Author Proposal form. All projects will be submitted to editorial review by external advisors.

SpringerBriefs are characterized by expedited production schedules with the aim for publication 8 to 12 weeks after acceptance and fast, global electronic dissemination through our online platform SpringerLink. The standard concise author contracts guarantee that

- an individual ISBN is assigned to each manuscript
- each manuscript is copyrighted in the name of the author
- the author retains the right to post the pre-publication version on his/her website or that of his/her institution.

More information about this series at http://www.springer.com/series/10082

C. Mantzavinos

A Dialogue on Institutions

Springer

C. Mantzavinos
Department of History and Philosophy of Science
University of Athens
Athens, Greece

ISSN 2211-4548 ISSN 2211-4556 (electronic)
SpringerBriefs in Philosophy
ISBN 978-3-030-63015-7 ISBN 978-3-030-63016-4 (eBook)
https://doi.org/10.1007/978-3-030-63016-4

This Springer imprint is published by the registered company Springer Nature Switzerland AG
The registered company address is: Gewerbestrasse 11, 6330 Cham, Switzerland

Γιά τήν Ἔλενα καί τόν Ἀλέξανδρο

Preface

Ideas are created, modified and crystallized before fading away—this process is accelerated when it occurs in a dialogical form. The dialogue is the philosophical method of acceleration in the world of ideas. This is the method I am using in the present work on institutions.

I am indebted to many friends, colleagues and students for their goodwill and support during the long gestation period of this dialogue. I would like to thank, especially for discussions or comments, Hans Albert, Jim Alt, Theodore Arabatzis, Darrell Arnold, Kosmas Brousalis, Gilles Campagnolo, Andrés Casas-Casas, Raine Daston, Gerd Gigerenzer, Aristides Hatzis, Nikolina Kamzola, Panagiotis Karadimas, Philip Kitcher, Roula Kitsiou, Alexander Linsbichler, Jonas Lipski, Uskali Mäki, Peter McLaughlin, Claude Ménard, Alexandros Mitsis-Koutoukis, Josiah Ober, Nikos Papaionannou, Evaggelos Pehas, Philip Pettit, Emmanuel Picavet, Panagiotis Thanassas, Dimitris Vassiliou, Stelios Virvidakis, Christian Walter and two anonymous reviewers.

I would also like to thank my editor at Springer, Christopher Wilby, for his support of the project.

The permission of the State Collection of Antiquities and Glyptothek Munich to reproduce the photograph by Renate Kühling of the statue of Eirene and Ploutos is kindly acknowledged.

Above all, I am indebted to my family, especially my wife Georgia, for her love and affection.

Athens, Greece
September 2020

C. Mantzavinos

Contents

Introduction

PABLO: How do you like *Casa Peter*?

STUDENT: Pablo, this is indeed a unique place! You were right to suggest that I stay here while in Cartagena.

PABLO: Lili and I have always found this place very atmospheric and we always recommend it to friends. This has been the former home of the American author and journalist Peter Tompkins…

STUDENT: Was he not the legendary secret service agent, quite active in World War II?

PABLO: Yes. He fell in love in Cartagena in the 70s and has bought this house, which is now run by his former employees.

STUDENT: No wonder that he wanted to buy a house in colonial Cartagena de Indias, right on the Caribbean coast. The view from the terrace on the Caribbean Sea, especially now during the sunset with all these beautiful colours in the sky is breathtaking!

PABLO: I am glad that you like it. Are you ready for a walk in the city?

STUDENT: Yes, let's go. Who would ever think that after spending so many years together in Germany we would meet again in Colombia? I am glad that after meeting you in Bogotá, I am now able to also meet you here in Cartagena.

PABLO: I was born in Bogotá and I love it very much, of course. People justly call it, I think, "the Athens of South America". But Cartagena, as you will see, has a thoroughly different flair.

STUDENT: I have been in three cities, in Bogotá, Medellín and Cartagena, so I am very glad to have had a chance to be acquainted with the diversity of this country.

PABLO: Yes, Bogotá is built at a high plateau in the Andes mountains, 2600 m above sea level and Cartagena at the Caribbean Sea.

STUDENT: And of course the eastern and southern portions of the country are tropical rainforest where small farming communities live, mostly indigenous people…

PABLO: …and where guerrillas and paramilitaries can easily hide!

C. Mantzavinos, *A Dialogue on Institutions*, SpringerBriefs in Philosophy,
https://doi.org/10.1007/978-3-030-63016-4_1

STUDENT: I have read that the country still has one of the highest homicide rates in the world; kidnapping was rife until very recently; and it is still a great center of the international drug industry. Assassinations of political leaders seem to be not uncommon and the combined fighting strength of non-state-armed forces, left-wing guerrillas, and paramilitaries was until recently approaching 50 percent of the size of the national army.[1]

PABLO: Yes. But the security situation in the last few years improved.

STUDENT: So, is there hope for a change in the trajectory of the country?

PABLO: President Uribe increased the size of the army and a sustained offensive pushed the principle rebel group, the Revolutionary Armed Forces of Colombia (FARC) out of half of the municipalities in which it was present in 2002.[2] But still, armed forces and paramilitaries are quite active, of course.

STUDENT: So, Colombia seems to be a sort of real-world laboratory to test the theoretical approaches to violence.

PABLO: Here speaks the social scientist! We were supposed to just have a walk in the city!

STUDENT: Of course, but why should this inhibit us from speaking about violence and institutions and all the issues that interest us since the time we were in Germany a few years ago?

PABLO: I see. Nothing seems to have changed in your interests since then! Still a young man interested in the ways the social world functions! Let me start by saying something obvious, if one takes the case of Colombia seriously: the definition of Max Weber that the state is an entity with a monopoly on the legitimate use of violence does not seem to be relevant here!

STUDENT: It depends, of course, on how you interpret the term *Gemeinschaft* in Max Weber's famous definition: "The state is that human *Gemeinschaft*, who within a certain territory—this: the territory, belongs to the distinctive feature—successfully lays claim to the monopoly of legitimate physical force for itself."[3]

PABLO: Independently of what Max Weber meant, it is important to stress that violence must be near the heart of any explanation of how societies function and evolve. The necessary prerequisite for forming durable large social groups is a way to control violence.

STUDENT: So, managing violence is the most fundamental problem societies face. This is what you are saying. This is nothing else than the Hobbesian problem of social order!

PABLO: That the interaction of self-interested individuals is bound to give rise to situations of social conflict is certainly the fundamental problem societies face—you can characterize it as the Hobbesian problem of social order, if you like, though most elements of Hobbes's solution, notably the construction of a social contract, belongs to fiction rather than to recorded history!

STUDENT: Hobbes's solution is not tenable, but the formulation of the problem is a valuable starting point, I think. Don't you agree?

PABLO: Let me refer to Douglass North, whose work both you and I respect so much. He insisted that independently of whether we analyze historical or modern societies, we must not assume that the state is a single coercive individual with a monopoly on violence.[4]

STUDENT: Yes, I know and he is right, of course. Violence is the outcome of the structure of the institutions, organizations and beliefs within a society. This structure also determines the degree of specialization in exerting violence.

PABLO: Exactly. The key is the consolidation of the military into one organization. But this does not emerge automatically. Much depends on how economic and political organizations have developed in the society that one is interested in. There must be a kind of balance between military and non military organizations.

STUDENT: I guess this is why it is so difficult to create and maintain a workable state in the long run—a double balance between military and nonmilitary organizations must be sustained!

PABLO: To put it bluntly, to understand the control of violence, we must begin with a group of powerful individuals and analyze how self-enforcing arrangements emerge that are effective in constraining them!

STUDENT: This is a very illuminating way to tackle the issue. From the impasse of the Hobbesian problem of social order rooted in the self-interested individual behavior and the resulting potential interindividual conflict, two exits seem to be possible.

PABLO: Which ones do you have in mind?

STUDENT: The first concerns the possibility of inventing and following social rules that may restrict the self-interested activity of all or nearly all of the members of society. The second is the realization of mutual advantage in exchange processes.

PABLO: Traditionally, the first solution is addressed by political theory; the second is usually the domain of economics.

STUDENT: Yes, indeed. Different authors have usually solved the problem of social order *either* by stressing the importance of formal and informal rules *or* by pointing to the division of labor and the gains of trade. I think that a more successful strategy for solving the Hobbesian problem of social order is simultaneously to analyze *both* aspects: the emergence of an order of general rules *and* the realization of the gains of trade within rules.

PABLO: I like the way you put the problem, but let me add to what you just said and give it a new twist: the fundamental problem that all societies face is how to survive in the face of uncertainty. There is a never-ending set of new problems, new challenges that require novel answers. These can be new illnesses like the recent coronavirus pandemics, security conflicts, economic crises, demographic changes and of course environmental challenges like climate change.

STUDENT: Collectively and individually coping with uncertainty—I agree.

PABLO: As North called it: Uncertainty in a non-ergodic world.[5]

STUDENT: Non-ergodicity as a constitutive condition of the fundamental problem of social order?

PABLO: An ergodic stochastic process simply means that averages calculated from past observations cannot be persistently different from the time average of future outcomes. So, non-ergodicity accordingly means that the states of affairs emerging in the future can be radically different from the state of affairs of the past.[6]

STUDENT: The social world is non-ergodic, a metaphysical assumption really!

PABLO: I don't think that North introduced non-ergodicity as a metaphysical assumption. For him the extraordinary changes in every facet of contemporary society are evident all around us; and it is evident that we have been and are creating societies that are unique in comparison to anything in the past!

STUDENT: Metaphysical or not, non-ergodicity as the starting point.

PABLO: North has elaborated the point as follows: "Many of the changes in the environment are novel, without precedent. The theories we have in the social sciences, however, are predicated on the notion of an ergodic, repeated and predictable world in which the same problems recur and individuals can fashion solutions to them. How do we think about social processes when individuals, at best, have a limited understanding of what is happening to them as they continue to confront new experiences and novel situations that require an awareness of the dynamic nature of the process of change in which they are participants? How do we deal with the new and novel problems that emerge as humans reshape the human environment in ways that have no historical precedent?"[7] He thought that we do not have an answer to these questions, although we acknowledge their importance.

STUDENT: Let me suggest the beginning of an answer, and you can correct me, if I am wrong.

PABLO: I can surely correct you: I am a Professor now, as you know!

STUDENT: Yes, I know. And I am very proud of you!

PABLO: I owe you so much. I have learned a lot from you during my time in Germany.

STUDENT: But now the roles have been reversed. I will be your student now!

PABLO: You have always been quite modest! But let us walk this way. If we take this street, we will reach the downtown of Cartagena.

The Problem Solving Approach to Institutions

STUDENT: Methodological individualism is my starting point, that is the methodological doctrine of starting any social analysis with the individual.[8] I think it is a fruitful strategy to start with the explanation of individual action and penetrate to the social phenomena to show that they are the result of interaction between individuals who follow their own interests according to their beliefs.

PABLO: Is this a good starting point? Let me remind you that John Searle in his own theory of institutions speaks of collective intentionality as the starting point.[9]

STUDENT: I know. His approach has become very influential in some philosophical circles, but it is hopelessly simplistic.

PABLO: But it is an extremely clear and systematic approach!

STUDENT: Clarity and systematicity do not substitute for truth and importance! Searle's approach is just a conceptual analysis which does not engage or take into consideration any findings of the social sciences. Developing a philosophical theory of institutions without paying any attention to the theories and empirical findings delivered by the social sciences is arrogant, if not simply comical!

PABLO: This is a stark attitude that you are adopting against a famous philosopher!

STUDENT: I think that I am just being fair. If someone pretends to provide the foundations of the social sciences without knowing or engaging with them, then he cannot claim my respect. What we need is philosophy of the social sciences, not such a parochial social philosophy which mostly offers banalities about the social world!

PABLO: Be that as it may! So you insist on adopting methodological individualism as a starting point. I take it that methodological individualism is different than both ontological individualism and political individualism.

STUDENT: Yes, that's right. I very much agree. It surely is different than the position that all that exists in the social world are individuals and from any position concerning the appropriate goal of politics. But it is also different than rational choice theory.

PABLO: In what sense?

STUDENT: The rationality postulate, either in its form as an internal consistency of choice or in its identification with the maximization of self-interest,[10] is different

C. Mantzavinos, *A Dialogue on Institutions*, SpringerBriefs in Philosophy,
https://doi.org/10.1007/978-3-030-63016-4_2

from methodological individualism in two ways. Firstly, methodological individualism is a proposal about how to formulate good theories of social phenomena. It can be more or less *fruitful* in leading social scientists towards good social scientific theories. Rational choice theory, in contrast, by design provides explanations of individuals' actual behavior. It is designed to be an *empirical theory or model* and so it can be true or false. Secondly, methodological individualism is a heuristic principle of a more general nature than the rationality principle: it contends that the analysis of individual behavior as the starting point is most important, regardless of its *concrete form*.

PABLO: I see. So, how do you use methodological individualism then?

STUDENT: The task is to provide an adequate explanation of individual behavior.

PABLO: What are the criteria of adequacy?

STUDENT: Mainly three. Firstly, that the analysis of individual behavior is a genuinely empirical one rather than an exercise in the pure logic of choice: logically coherent models of choice that are empirically irrelevant clearly will not do. Secondly, dynamic aspects of behavior must be taken into consideration: since individuals are the bearers of social and economic change, only if changes in their behavior can be accounted for can the interaction between them also generate a socioeconomic change. Finally, the third criterion of adequacy is that the analysis of individual behavior should take into consideration the differences in behavior among individuals: this is the issue of subjectivism, i.e. that every person possesses a uniqueness manifested in his individual history, deeds, and thoughts.

PABLO: I am curious to hear which account can accomplish all that!

STUDENT: Haha! You are right, this is exactly the challenge, but think of this: if we treat individual behavior in a problem solving framework, I believe we could accomplish this.

PABLO: But let me ask you here: what is a problem?

STUDENT: I would say that a person is confronted with a problem when he wants something and does not know immediately what series of actions he can perform to get it. The desired object may be very tangible, let's say an apple to eat or quite abstract such as an elegant proof of a theorem. It may be specific, for example that particular apple over there or quite general, for example something to appease hunger. It may be a physical object like an apple or a set of symbols like the proof of a theorem. The actions involved in obtaining desired objects include physical actions like walking, reaching, writing, perceptual activities like looking, listening, and purely mental activities like judging the similarity of two symbols, remembering a scene, and so on.[11]

PABLO: One can define a problem by an initial state, by one or more goal states to be reached, by a set of operators that can transform one state into another, and by constraints that a solution must meet.[12] The procedure of problem solving can be perceived as a method of applying operators so that the goal states can be reached.

STUDENT: This problem solving framework is appropriate when accounting for individual behavior because of its general applicability.

PABLO: But you must be more specific in order to be convincing!

STUDENT: Yes, of course. Here is the suggestion. For any explanation of individual behavior you need two kinds of assumptions, a motivational and a cognitive one.

PABLO: Psychologists subsume very different things under 'motivation', so that the concept is often vacuous. You should specify it further!

STUDENT: You are right. For our purpose, a general motivation that is empirical and operational enough to be employed in social theory will suffice. I propose therefore the following hypothesis: every individual strives for an increase in his or her own utility.

PABLO: Isn't this the hypothesis that the Scottish moral philosophers of the eighteenth century first put forward?

STUDENT: Indeed. Adam Ferguson thought that man is in some measure the artificer of his own frame and of his own fortune and is always improving on his subject carrying the intention everywhere "through the streets of the populous city, or the wilds of the forest."[13]

STUDENT: And Adam Smith has written in the *Wealth of Nations*, if I remember correctly, about the principle which prompts to save that it "is the desire of bettering our condition, a desire which though generally calm and dispassionate, comes with us from the womb, and never leaves us till we go into the grave."[14]

PABLO: So, the attainment of utility is the ultimate problem of the individual.

STUDENT: Yes. And this leaves open what the concrete content of this utility is for every individual. Every person considers and pursues utility in a different way.

PABLO: And this is where the second assumption comes in, I guess.

STUDENT: Exactly. The cognitive assumption which views the mind as the product of a long evolutionary process during which phylogenetic learning that is species specific unfolds and sets the framework of possibilities within which every member of the species can acquire its learning history, that is, ontogenetic knowledge. From the amoeba to Einstein the growth of knowledge is the same, according to Popper's famous dictum.[15]

PABLO: Our brain can solve problems inherent in the environment in which it exists and is forced to survive—it is constructed to solve adaptive problems.[16]

STUDENT: Without wanting to go into the debate on the relationship between brain and mind and whether the mind should be viewed as a general problem solver or as a set of specialized problem solvers…

PABLO: …as evolutionary psychologists insist.[17]

STUDENT: Yes. It is only important to keep in mind that biological evolution is a very slow process, whereas the modern world emerged within an evolutionary eye-blink, so that there is certainly a tension between our biological-cognitive make up and the environment of the modern world in which we must survive.

PABLO: Yes, that's right. Biological evolution has functionally prepared us to solve the particular distribution of problems that were characteristic of humans' hunter-gatherer past, rather than those problems that are faced in a context where people remain concentrated in front of a computer screen for many hours!

STUDENT: Although this is certainly the case, it is also the case that there has hardly been any change in the biological make up of Homo sapiens for over 30,000 years, so there is an invariance here.

PABLO: This makes at least some things easier to think about.

STUDENT: For our purposes, it is sufficient to conceptualize mental activity as problem solving activity, viewing a great range of mental phenomena like perception, attention, reasoning and learning within a problem solving framework.

PABLO: So, cognition and problem solving, this is our topic for now. But listen!

STUDENT: Listen what?

PABLO: This is a traditional Colombian song.

STUDENT: Where does the music come from?

PABLO: From the band which is playing in front of the statue of Botero. We have reached the Plaza de Santo Domingo.

STUDENT: This is a very lively Plaza, indeed very beautiful. Incidentally, this was a good example of pragmatic cognition. Exactly like in the case in which I would tell you: "Observe!" You would then immediately ask back: "Observe what?" There is no perception per se, but always a perception relevant to a problem situation.

PABLO: Yes, cognitive science suggests that we view the mind as a complex structure that actively interprets and, at the same time, classifies the varied signals received by the senses—from the physical environment and from the sociocultural-linguistic environment.[18] A wide variety of mental representations have been offered as cognitive models to describe the mental operations at work.[19]

STUDENT: I think that you most probably agree that the pragmatic notion of mental models seems to be the most appropriate for the explanatory purposes here. Mental models gradually evolve during our cognitive development to organize our perceptions and keep track of our memories. A mental model can be best understood as the final prediction that the mind makes or as an expectation that it has regarding the environment before getting feedback from it. Depending on whether the expectation formed is validated by the environmental feedback, the mental model can be revised, refined, or rejected altogether.[20]

PABLO: And learning is the complex modification of the mental models according to the feedback received from the environment.

STUDENT: Problem solving on the basis of mental models is, of course, a process prone to errors. The testing of solutions to problems in the environment does not necessarily lead to success. The opposite is the case—we make mistakes all the time, but we are able to correct them and to learn from our mistakes.

PABLO: Trial-and-error!

STUDENT: Would you say that theoretical knowledge exhausts all human knowledge?

PABLO: No, of course not: "knowing how" is as important as "knowing that". The important thing is that we also acquire all our skills and dexterities by trial-and-error when solving practical problems in the environment.

STUDENT: As in the famous example of Gilbert Ryle, winning battles: A soldier does not become a shrewd general merely by endorsing the strategic principles of Clausewitz; he must also be competent to apply them. Knowing how to apply maxims cannot be reduced to, or derived from, the acceptance of those or any other maxims.[21]

PABLO: Indeed. Know how consists of the capacity to act according to rules which are overt enough to be discovered and followed but which cannot always be stated in words.[22]

STUDENT: This distinction has been recently challenged by some philosophers, I think.[23] But wasn't Ryle essentially right in the end? He refuted the intellectualist legend according to which to act while thinking of what one is doing is always to do two things at the same time, namely to consider certain appropriate propositions, or prescriptions, and to put into practice what these propositions or prescriptions enjoin. It is to do a bit of theory and then to do a bit of practice.[24]

PABLO: I do not know what these philosophers are saying, but given the mountains of evidence from cognitive science, the distinction between theoretical knowledge and practical knowledge, between knowing that and knowing how, seems to be indisputable!

STUDENT: I am glad that you agree that Ryle's point remains convincing and that efficient practice precedes the theory of it. It was because Aristotle found himself and others reasoning now intelligently now stupidly that he was able to provide the maxims and prescriptions of logic.[25]

PABLO: Now, all that is fairly old and well-known. Have you been able to come up with anything new? What interests me my dear friend is what are your own ideas and thoughts and not those of others!

STUDENT: My main idea is to introduce a distinction between old problems and new problems. This distinction does not hinge upon the main characteristic of all individual knowledge, which is its conjectural nature. Even when a problem has often been tested in the environment, and it has been solved in the same way many times in the past so that the solution has become so standardized as to become an unconscious routine, its conjectural character remains intact.

PABLO: The possibility of error always remains, I hope you would not doubt this?

STUDENT: No, I agree: the possibility of error always remains. Now, every time that an individual is confronted with a problem situation, he is, literally speaking, faced with a novel situation. When perceiving the natural and socio-cultural environment, the human mind actively interprets and classifies it.[26] In a certain sense a new cognitive achievement takes place every time. However, the classification process in which the mind engages itself presupposes that available classes already exist under which the current input of the environment can be classified. When these classes do in fact exist, we can speak of the relevant problem solution as an "old problem."

PABLO: I see.

STUDENT: If the current problem is identified as a familiar one—in the sense that it can be classified in an existing class—then the appropriate solution will be applied automatically in the form of a rule. In other words, whenever our cognitive system comparing the current problem situation with past problem situations stored and classified in the memory finds that it is of the same type, it then automatically applies the corresponding solution designated by the respective class. In these cases we can speak of old problems.

PABLO: I see, whenever our mind classifies a situation as an old one, an existing problem situation that has worked successfully in the past is automatically triggered. Would this then mean that on the behavioral level we will then tend to follow unconscious routines?

STUDENT: Exactly. But obviously, not all problems are of this kind. Whenever an old problem solution no longer works—possibly because of a change in the environment—or whenever a problem situation, when compared to past problem situations stored in the human mind, cannot be classified under any familiar type or class, we speak of a "new problem." In other words, if the mental model of the problem space currently constructed by an individual is essentially new in its characteristics, so that no ready-made solution to the problem is available, it then constitutes a new problem for the individual.

PABLO: But all the old problems of an individual were new at some point in its history. I guess you agree on this?

STUDENT: Of course.

PABLO: What happens when an individual conceives of a situation as a new problem?

STUDENT: There are two subsequent kinds of responses. The first response to the new problem is quasi-automatic. It involves the employment of so-called inferential strategies.[27]

PABLO: Do you mean all these processes of inference that we know from psychology? Inferential problems such as the description and characterization of events, the detection of covariation among events, causal inference, prediction, etc. are normally solved by laypersons with the aid of judgmental strategies or "heuristics."

STUDENT: Yes, heuristics are general strategies that provide quick solutions with little effort. Gerd Gigerenzer has famously discovered a large number of fast and frugal heuristics "that make us smart."[28] He goes so far to argue that the mind is an adaptive toolbox consisting of heuristics.[29]

PABLO: It was high time to move away from "algorithms," the methodical procedures that guarantee success by solving problems through their lengthy, patient application.

STUDENT: So, when confronted with a new problem, inferential strategies are triggered in our endeavour to solve it. The most powerful one is certainly analogy[30]: if I know how to ride a bicycle and I sit for the first time on a motorcycle, I try to balance the same way as when I sit on a bicycle.

PABLO: But inferential strategies are normally used in the context of theoretical knowledge, that is knowledge which has largely a propositional structure, right?

STUDENT: Yes, this is the common usage. However, as my example has just shown, analogies are also inferential strategies—of a broader type to be sure—that can be applied to practical knowledge.

PABLO: I see. But inferential strategies do not guarantee success. I guess you do not want to claim that?

STUDENT: Heuristics, inferential strategies, may lead to errors, of course. There is nothing that guarantees success in solving the new problem. The important thing to acknowledge is only that when faced with a new problem, our cognitive system mobilizes cognitive resources to solve it from *those that already exist*. Our mind loves to make inferences.[31] We even tend to generalize from just one case, and if we avail of a satisfactory solution to a problem in one domain, an analogical transfer is triggered to a very different domain.

PABLO: And we might succeed or fail.

STUDENT: If we succeed, we will tend to reapply the same solution to this problem the next time and again and again as long as we are successful.

PABLO: And if we fail?

STUDENT: The cognitive system registers this failure and the subsequent second stage is introduced—a deliberation and choice process in the light of consciousness.

PABLO: I hope that you do not now want to offer a theory of consciousness as well!

STUDENT: No, I do not need that! All I claim is that the cognitive system informed by the current environmental situation and interpreting it as a new problem, and after the quick inferential strategies have proved unsuccessful, engages in what we call in ordinary language "reflection." This deliberation process is nothing more than a mental probing of alternatives. It is the mental state which can be best described in ordinary terms as the generation of candidates for providing a solution to the new choice problem.

PABLO: So, choice is tied here to the notion of the solution of a new problem. Is this what you are claiming?

STUDENT: Yes. When everything else on which the mind can draw upon has failed, a choice is made.

PABLO: But isn't it a rational choice, after all? The one you said you did not agree with?

STUDENT: No, not at all! It is the case that the deliberation process, during which the alternatives are created and the choice is made, occurs in the light of consciousness.[32] But the conscious reflection on alternatives and the subsequent choice do not imply that the alternatives are created in any predetermined way.

PABLO: But you do not want to imply either, I hope, that the alternatives are created following the principle of random or blind mutation?

STUDENT: No, of course not.

PABLO: I say that, because you seem to favor evolutionary epistemology and there it is common to assume that going beyond what is already known, one cannot but go blindly—this is consistent with the principles of biological evolution.[33]

STUDENT: Yes, I know. But though I share the unconditional notion of choice, conscious creation and reflection on alternatives that human minds engage in is definitely categorically different than what is going on in the evolution of animals.

PABLO: I think you must say more about choice processes. I am not convinced.

STUDENT: Yes, in a minute. But let me complete the picture of the problem solving framework first.

PABLO: I'm listening!

STUDENT: So, when everything else has failed, choice takes place in an attempt to solve the "new problem." When faced with a new problem, and while generating alternatives in the process of deliberation, the individual possesses in any case one possible alternative way to solve the new problem: to acquire ready-made solutions from the environment.

PABLO: I see; the mind creates novel alternatives, one of which is always to acquire ready-made solutions directly from others.

STUDENT: Yes. In an imaginative process, the individual mind devises new alternatives. Creativity is thus a property of the human mind, which is employed when working out new alternatives in order to solve a new problem.

PABLO: And the created solution is then tried out in the environment....

STUDENT: ...and it can be either successful or not.

PABLO: If it is successful?

STUDENT: Then this chosen alternative will be reinforced and the next time that this problem arises, the same solution will be reapplied. After it has been employed successfully many times, the solution will be standardized and will become a routine. In other words, the individual will avail herself of a ready-made solution to the problem, and thus every time she is confronted with it, it will be classified as an "old problem" and dealt with unconsciously.

PABLO: I see; this is how the routinization of behavior is explained in your framework.

STUDENT: Exactly.

PABLO: And what happens if the novel problem solution fails?

STUDENT: Then a new creative choice process starts anew.

PABLO: I see.

STUDENT: I have written down all this in a figure with the essential ingredients of the problem solving framework. Let us make a pause and sit down on the bench, so that I can show it to you...

PABLO: We have reached the Plaza de Bolivar. Let us look for a bench there and make a pause.

STUDENT: Here it is. I have written it down in my notebook.[34]

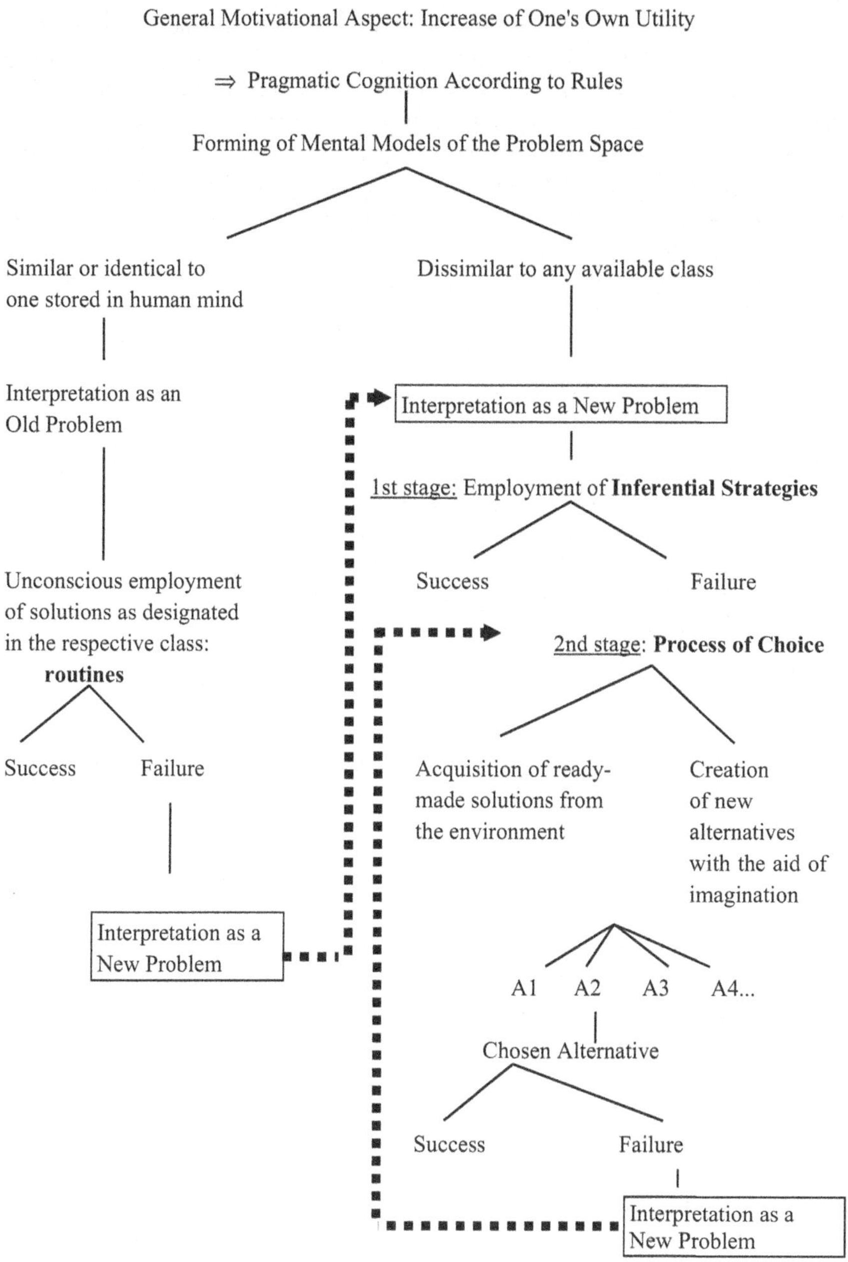
General Motivational Aspect: Increase of One's Own Utility
⇒ Pragmatic Cognition According to Rules
Forming of Mental Models of the Problem Space
Similar or identical to one stored in human mind
Dissimilar to any available class
Interpretation as an Old Problem
Interpretation as a New Problem
1st stage: Employment of Inferential Strategies
Unconscious employment of solutions as designated in the respective class: routines
Success
Failure
2nd stage: Process of Choice
Success
Failure
Acquisition of ready-made solutions from the environment
Creation of new alternatives with the aid of imagination
Interpretation as a New Problem
A1
A2
A3
A4...
Chosen Alternative
Success
Failure
Interpretation as a New Problem

PABLO: I can see how this works. However, I am not convinced yet that what you say about choice is really different than the standard rational choice account.

STUDENT: There are similarities, of course, but also differences. Before I elaborate on them, let me clarify something at the outset. I think that we should not concentrate our efforts on whether a choice is perfectly *rational*, boundedly *rational*, hyper-*rational* etc. This is not very fruitful. The question of *rationality*, though of obvious importance, is of a normative character and does not need to concern us here. What we are after is a workable explanation of choice processes with empirical content, not of normative models of *rationality*.

PABLO: I agree with that.

STUDENT: Now, the choice process that I outlined consists of two subsequent stages: the creation of alternatives with the aid of imagination and the evaluation of alternatives—also with the aid of imagination.

PABLO: You seem to put a lot of stress on imagination and creativity!

STUDENT: Yes, and this is the difference from standard accounts. Choice is always forward looking and is a purely speculative operation. In the words of G.L.S. Shackle, choice is a beginning, an uncaused cause and therefore a genuinely creative act.[35] Choice can only be "choice of thoughts of deeds."[36]

PABLO: Yes, but in the second stage of the evaluation of alternatives, the agent will choose according to the general motivation to increase his or her own utility—isn't that right?

STUDENT: Yes, but here again imagination is also at work: the imagination of future alternative degrees of satisfaction. The individual assigns to the alternatives different values according to how much utility each alternative is expected to offer upon realization. The imagination, thus, also functions as a way of assigning utility values to alternatives expected to occur in a future moment of time.

PABLO: But this is what rational choice theory also postulates: ordering of alternatives, attaching values to them and choosing the one expected to yield the highest value!

STUDENT: Yes, but remember we are operating within a more general problem solving framework, which can accommodate both simpler and more complex cases. For example, the simplest variant of rational choice theory is obviously the choice under certainty, that is, the situation in which the agent possessing a well-defined utility function can order actions and outcomes in such a way that picking the utility-maximizing alternative seems entirely possible. For example, in microeconomics textbooks, the individual chooser is presented as a set of indifference curves with a budget restriction, and her rational choice consists of selecting the consumption bundle that maximizes her marginal utility. This explanation is *not empirically wrong*. The issue is rather that this theory can be applied only in a very small number of cases and it thus has very little empirical content. In my framework, this consumer choice under certainty can be easily incorporated as a subcase of the solution to an exceptionally *well-defined problem*. The problem space is conceived and interpreted by the agent in an unambiguous way since the "objects perceived," that is prices, quantities, qualities, etc. are easily identifiable physical entities. Therefore the agent is able to choose easily and with great exactitude the best alternative and proceed to its subsequent trial in order to solve her new problem.

PABLO: The trouble is that in a non-ergodic world, most problems are ill-defined! To adapt Tolstoy's remark about happy and unhappy families, well-defined problems are all alike, but every ill-defined problem is ill-defined in its own way![37] In a world of genuine uncertainty, that is in the real world, fuzzy, ill-defined sorts of problems abound in everyday life!

STUDENT: Exactly. The real world is the world of "genuine uncertainty" not of "parametric uncertainty." Introducing into the analysis subjective probabilities that agents are supposed to be able to assign to the different possible outcomes of their action and then maximize their utility is simply not possible under conditions of genuine uncertainty. This is my point.

PABLO: The main issue is simply this: the assignment of subjective probabilities cannot transform uncertainty into calculable certainty. Calculable risk has, of course, nothing to do with genuine uncertainty—we know this since Frank Knight![38]

STUDENT: The assumption that probability that in some sense can yield a numerical basis for calculation can turn essential unknowledge into knowledge is inherently self-contradictory. When someone says he is uncertain what he usually means is not that he just does not know the probabilities of various outcomes, but that he does not even know what outcomes are possible!

PABLO: Yes, that is why the evaluation of alternatives, your second stage of the choice process can never be accurate in any sense! I will tell you an anecdote about a famous decision theorist. Sidney Morgenbesser, a professor of philosophy at Columbia University, used to tell a story about meeting Luce, the coauthor of a standard work in formal decision-making models. He had received a job offer from another university and was considering it. He asked Sidney Morgenbesser what he should do. He responded that he was an expert on formal decision making models, so he should surely know better. "Come on" he said, "this is serious!"

STUDENT: This is great!

PABLO: It is, isn't it?

STUDENT: And here is a story from Darwin's autobiography. A couple of years after completion of his historic scientific voyage on the Beagle, Charles Darwin, then 29 years old, had started considering his personal life and he wrote the following notes in pencil on a scrap of paper with the heading: "This is the Question," divided into two columns like a balance sheet. I have kept it in my notebook. Here it is[39]:

MARRY	Not MARRY
Children—(if it please God)—constant companion, (friend in old age) who will feel interested in one, object to be beloved and played with—better than a dog anyhow—Home, and someone to take care of house—Charms of music and female chit-chat. These things good for one's health. Forced to visit and receive relations *but terrible loss of time* My God, it is intolerable to think of spending one's whole life, like a neuter bee, working, working and nothing after all.— No, no won't do.— Imagine living all one's day solitarily in smoky dirty London House.—Only picture to yourself a nice soft wife on a sofa with good fire, and books and music perhaps—compare this vision with the dingy reality of Grt Marlboro' St.	No children, (no second life) no one to care for one in old age.— What is the use of working without sympathy from near and dear friends—who are near and dear friends to the old except relatives. Freedom to go where one liked—Choice of Society *and little of it*. Conversation of clever men at clubs.—Not forced to visit relatives, and to bend in every trifle—to have the expense and anxiety of children—perhaps quarrelling *Loss of time*—cannot read in the evenings—fatness and idleness —anxiety and responsibility—less money for books etc.—if many children forced to gain one's bread.—(But then it is very bad for one's health to work too much) Perhaps my wife won't like London; then the sentence is banishment and degradation with indolent idle fool—

The young Darwin decided that he should marry and hc wrote "Marry-Marry-Marry Q.E.D." beneath the first column. On the reverse side of the page he considered what his decision would mean with respect to his freedom: "There is many a happy slave." The following year he married his cousin, Emma Wedgwood, with whom he had 10 children.

PABLO: 10 children!

STUDENT: A happy slave indeed!

PABLO: Nice story! Let's take stock now. Where are we? Why is the problem solving framework important after all?

STUDENT: It is important for the explanatory purposes of the social sciences because it overcomes the two main behavioral models in the social sciences, *Homo oeconomicus* and *Homo sociologicus*. The standard model used by economists assumes that agents are guided in their behavior by a case-by-case maximization of their utility function. The standard model used by sociologists assumes that agent's behavior is dictated by social norms. *Homo oeconomicus* is forward-looking, intentional, and responsive to incentives. *Homo sociologicus* is pushed from behind by quasi-inertial forces and follows rules blindly.

PABLO: According to a famous dictum: "Economics is all about how people make choices; Sociology is all about why they don't have any choices to make!"[40]

STUDENT: Exactly! The preference of economists for the rational utility maximizer is due to their traditional primary focus: market exchange and price formation. The main idea of the subjective theory of value, one of the greatest achievements of economics, since the marginal revolution of the 1870s has been the conclusion that prices are formed in an exchange process, taking place after the agents have ordered their preferences and have decided which goods they want to exchange.

PABLO: And then of course this behavioral model has also been applied to politics, law, family, and what have you. This is economics imperialism.[41]

STUDENT: Yes. The preference of the sociologists for modelling the agent as a norm follower is due to their own special theoretical interest. The Durkheim-Parsons tradition in sociology sought to find a satisfactory solution to the Hobbesian problem of social order without invoking utilitarian considerations. Norm-guided behavior seemed to be the proper model to explain the maintenance of a workable social order.

PABLO: And your problem solving framework incorporates both kinds of behavior.

STUDENT: Since individuals are supposed to be able to learn by experience in an uncertain environment, it is plausible that a behavioral regularity is shown whenever old problems arise or when recurring situations take place. The behavioral regularity is the essential characteristic of an enlightened *Homo sociologicus*. Such regularity allows for continuity of behavior; and this continuity distinguishes *Homo sociologicus* from all those sociological views that suggest that behavior is merely the effect of hidden occult social forces.

PABLO: But the enlightened *Homo sociologicus* is only part of the story, I guess.

STUDENT: Of course. There are many problem situations that the individual is unable to classify as similar and, thus, for which he is unable to employ automatically and unconsciously the appropriate solution designated for the respective class. These cases form the new problems for the individual; and as a consequence he is forced to reflect and choose before acting. The individual's choice is not always a utility-maximizing one, as assumed by the rational choice model, but rather a human choice based on his imaginative faculties. This reflection process concerning the solution of a new problem is essential for an enlightened *Homo oeconomicus*.

PABLO: The upshot of the discussion seems to be that the problem solving model incorporates both aspects of behavior, the case of problem classification and subsequent behavioral regularity and the case of reflective choice and subsequent novel behavior. The transition from novelty to routinization seems to be the universal cycle of our inner world—the rhythm of our mental processes unfolding on various time scales.[42]

STUDENT: Exactly. The prime difficulty for an external observer is to discern whether the agent perceives the situation as a familiar one or as a new one. When the observer can ascertain that the agent will interpret a problem situation as a familiar one, he can then predict that the agent will behave the same way as in the past. If the observer ascertains that the problem situation possesses a novel character in the eyes of the agent, then he can only predict that the agent will first employ some inferential strategies, and if they do not work, he will create a set of alternatives and choose the one that he will judge as most conducive to his utility. Obviously, misinterpretations may occur on the part of the agent, that is, classification errors that are bound to puzzle an observer. In these cases, the predictions regarding the behavior of the agent are bound, by an external observer, to be proved false—these cases are the "anomalies" of behavior.

PABLO: I see. And you say that this model satisfies all three criteria of adequacy for an explanation of individual behavior for the purposes of social theory?

STUDENT: Yes, it is an empirical one—not an exercise in logic, that is. It accounts for dynamic aspects of human behavior and allows for subjectivism, that is the huge variety of human behavior.

PABLO: And the great benefit of this approach is, of course, that you have found a consistent way to integrate beliefs into the behavioral model.

STUDENT: Exactly. When environmental feedback confirms the same mental model many times, it becomes stabilized in a way. This relatively crystallized mental model is a "belief." And we can call the interconnection of beliefs which can be either consistent or inconsistent a "belief system."

PABLO: But the next step should be to move to the level of society.

STUDENT: Exactly. Learning at the social level can be best conceptualized as collective learning, I think. When we want to say something sensible about the emergence of social or cultural knowledge, we must distinguish between two aspects of collective learning, the static and the evolutionary one.

PABLO: Yes, and the analysis of communication plays a fundamental role during which shared mental models are formed.[43]

STUDENT: Shared mental models provide the framework for a common interpretation of reality, I agree.

PABLO: And they give rise to collective solutions to the problems arising in the environment: a common interpretation of reality is the foundation of any further social interaction.

STUDENT: But the most interesting aspect of collective learning is how shared mental models evolve over time, I think. Don't you agree?

PABLO: Of course, I do.

STUDENT: Collective learning seems to depend crucially on the group size and is therefore different within organizations and in the society at large. Shared learning first takes place within families, neighborhoods, and schools, that is, within organizations. Systems of distributed cognition emerge and function within organizations.[44] But what is more important to understand is what is going on at the level of society. Throughout human history witchcraft, magic, and religions have been dominant. Behavior characterized by dogmas, prejudices, and "half-baked" theories has driven the historical process.

PABLO: Walking past the Palace of Inquisition let me show you the "Window of Denunciation" on the side wall, around the corner of the main entrance. Here it is. This small window with the simple crucifix above it bears the legend "Ventana de la Denuncia". At this small aperture on the side of the building pious folk could drop off anonymous missives denouncing their neighbors at Satan's spawn!

STUDENT: But only the members of the Spanish Inquisition were well equipped to express judgments about so important issues such as what constitutes magic, blasphemy and heresy, I guess. Right?

PABLO: Not quite. It was the Court of the Holy Office really which expressed such judgments. And these judgments were based on solid evidence. The experiment conducted was the following: The person accused of witchcraft was placed onto a giant scale which is still available inside the building, if you want to inspect it. Depending on how much she weighed, the Court of the Holy Office could objectively judge whether a woman was a witch or not and how powerful a witch she was.

STUDENT: But I am sure that the accused persons did have a chance to present the Court of the Holy Office *arguments* in their defense?

PABLO: Of course. The procedure was standardized, so that all defendants could be treated equally and get a fair trial. All of them had a choice to provide answers to a series of questions including: "How did you become a witch and what happened on that occasion?", "What words do you pronounce when you fly?" and "Do you fly fast?"

STUDENT: Apparently, Cartagena was full of witches in the 17th and 18th century.

PABLO: Indeed. Over 800 trials took place by the Holy Office and as far as I know, not a single person was ever found innocent.

STUDENT: Which speaks for the efficiency of the whole procedure!

PABLO: Humans theorize in the face of uncertainty all the time—and their behavior is guided by "half-baked" theories, i.e. by fallible, often erroneous beliefs which evolve over time.

STUDENT: "Half-baked" theories, this is a nice way to put it! In any case, these beliefs are shaped in a process of collective learning. They range from ad hoc views and loosely structured ideas such as those encompassed in the labels "conservative" and "liberal" to elegant systematic ideologies such as Marxism or organized religions. And the process of collective learning is closely connected with the process of cultural evolution, of course.

STUDENT: And I think that it is very important to stress that it is not only theoretical knowledge, that is knowledge communicable by means of natural and artificial symbols that matters.

PABLO: In other words, it is not only the stock of theoretical knowledge transmitted from generation to generation that matters—scientific knowledge is the most prominent example in modern times. The other category of knowledge that we have been talking about earlier, practical knowledge or "know how," is equally important. This is not always easily, if at all, transmissible in linguistic terms to others; the mechanism of its transmission is rather the direct imitation of the performance of others. Practical knowledge encompasses all skills acquired by solving practical problems—swimming, cooking, riding a bicycle, driving a car etc.—and is equally important for the everyday life of all individuals in a society.[45]

STUDENT: And Hayek was the first to argue about the immense importance of our evolved capacities,[46] which emerged in a very long process of trial-and-error rather than in a process of "rational justification." As he nicely put it, if I remember correctly: "If we stopped doing everything for which we do not know the reason, or for which we cannot provide a justification […] we would probably very soon be dead."[47]

PABLO: For Hayek the growth of knowledge includes our habits and skills, our emotional attitudes, our tools, and our institutions. They are all adaptations to past experience which have grown up by selective elimination of less suitable conduct.[48]

STUDENT: That minds do not create institutions, but that minds and institutions evolve together seems to be the main message of Hayek. But we need to develop a more analytic understanding of how shared mental models, collective learning, and institutions are connected. And this is what I am after. I met Douglass North in St. Louis once and he used to say that he had spent his whole life studying institutions and if he had reached any kind of theoretical insights, it is because he had used some definitions and distinctions which have proved to be very useful. So, here is the most important one: institutions are the rules of the game in a society that structure human interaction. They consist of formal rules (constitutions, statutes and common law, and regulations), informal rules, and the enforcement characteristics of each. Because they make up the incentive structure of a society, they define the way the game is played through time.[49]

PABLO: Yes, this is broadly accepted today.

STUDENT: But institutions do not merely provide incentives to the players of the game. They themselves enable them to solve a variety of problems that they encounter in their environment. This is the very point of stressing the cognitive dimension of human behavior!

PABLO: Of course, my dear friend, nobody denies this!

STUDENT: I disagree. All rational choice theorists do deny this! For them institutions are nothing else than yet another constraint. Depending on their content, they can induce or inhibit action.

PABLO: But I do not think that the two views are inconsistent.

STUDENT: Here is how I want to think about it. When theorizing about institutions it is useful to distinguish between two aspects: external and internal. From an external point of view, institutions are shared behavioral regularities or shared routines within a population. From an internal point of view, they are nothing more than shared solutions to recurrent problems of social interaction…

PABLO: … based on shared mental models, of course.

STUDENT: Yes, and it is only because institutions are anchored in people's minds that they ever become behaviorally relevant! It is the elucidation of the internal aspect that makes up the crucial step towards adequately explaining the emergence, evolution, and effects of institutions. This makes for the qualitative difference between a cognitive approach to institutions and other approaches.

PABLO: But a rational choice is also a cognitive process!

STUDENT: I admit that. Rational choice does shed some light on cognitive processes, but it does so in a very standardized way, putting all mental phenomena on the Prokrustean bed of a rational choice!

PABLO: This is probably the case, but it is still vastly more productive than just theorizing in terms of structures, aggregates, and social wholes!

STUDENT: Anyway, my point is that we should not lose track of the phenomenon that institutions are a means of unburdening individuals from permanently making decisions. By defining general normative patterns of behavior shared by individuals, they free individuals from the need to decide each time anew. This relief provided by institutions is productive because it releases the individual's energies to concentrate on other creative enterprises.[50] The advancement of civilization is due to the increase of the number of important operations which we can perform without thinking about them. Whitehead likened operations of thought with "cavalry charges in a battle—they are strictly limited in number, they require fresh horses, and must only be made at decisive moments!"[51]

PABLO: You can stress the enabling aspect of institutions, if you like, but this is not equivalent to neglecting their fundamental effect of providing incentives for action!

STUDENT: Before coming to the effect of institutions, let me clarify something first.

PABLO: I don't know what you want to clarify, but here is the other distinction that North asked that we respect, the one between institutions and organizations.

STUDENT: Of course.

PABLO: Institutions are the rules of the game; organizations are the players. The latter consist of groups of individuals bound together by some common objective. For example, firms are economic organizations, political parties are political organizations, and universities are educational organizations.

STUDENT: This is an extremely important distinction, I agree. But organizations are not the only players of the game—individuals are also players.

PABLO: Of course.

STUDENT: Now, let us pose the simple question: why do institutions exist?

PABLO: They exist because they provide the means of solving social problems and overcoming social conflict. This is their most fundamental raison d' être.

STUDENT: The life of man in a society without institutions would be in the phrase of Hobbes "solitary, poore, nasty, brutish and short."[52]

PABLO: You seem to like Hobbes a lot, but let me remind you of the obvious: social order does not need to arise only when formal institutions enforced by a state exist; social order also exists when people share merely informal institutions, like moral rules and social norms. In fact, human groups survived for thousands of years without any kind of state as an enforcement agency.

STUDENT: So, institutions exist because they provide the solution to problems of interindividual conflict. This has something to do with the motivational side of individual behavior that we have been discussing: the striving of the individuals to better their condition, to increase their utility. But there is another class of reasons explaining the existence of institutions, and this has to do with the cognitive architecture of humans. This is what I am saying!

PABLO: I do not disagree with that!

STUDENT: I ask: why do people agree on or accept institutions, that is, social normative rules, rather than deciding each time anew on particular norms regulating the particular conflict every time it arises?

PABLO: Why?

STUDENT: It is because we are limited in our cognitive capacities. We mobilize our energies only when a new problem arises and follow routines when we classify the problem situation as a familiar one. Because of the limited computational capacity of our minds, we tend not to solve social problems ad hoc every time they arise, but to the degree that they are recurrent and stylized, we adopt standardized solutions that we employ unconsciously.

PABLO: Rules in general are a device for coping with our "constitutional ignorance"; they are the device we have learned to use because our reason is insufficient to master the full detail of complex reality.[53]

STUDENT: At a more general level, the release of energies provided by institutions makes the very development of the individuality and personality of humans possible.

PABLO: One cannot develop a unique personality in all areas of life!

STUDENT: So, this is why institutions exist. Once there, they have a major effect: they stabilize expectations and thus reduce the uncertainty of the agents.

PABLO: The world is an uncertain place. Institutions provide a first structuring of the environment, a first more or less secure approximation of what will happen and what will not, and what will probably appear and what will not.

STUDENT: How do institutions emerge?

PABLO: I guess God has written them down and handed them over to our ancestors and so we have them now!

STUDENT: But how do we know that this has happened?

PABLO: But they are written down my dear friend—in Holy Scriptures that everybody can read!

STUDENT: Here is a more realistic answer: there are two main mechanisms of institutional emergence. They emerge either deliberately or spontaneously, that is either as a product of collective action or as a product of a spontaneous process of social interaction.

PABLO: And it is, of course, the case that the deliberate creation of institutions is more easily to come to grips with; it is more problematic to record their spontaneous emergence, crystallizing the unintended social repercussions of intentional human actions.

STUDENT: And I should add that the emergence of informal and formal institutions is driven by distinct mechanisms, don't you agree? A society's informal institutions emerge and change in a process of spontaneous interaction and are "indeed the result of human action, but not the execution of any human design," as Ferguson put it.[54]

PABLO: Indeed. The question is only: how can you apply your problem solving model to delineate such processes?

STUDENT: Here it is: An individual perceives his situation as constituting a new problem because the environment has changed, and after an act of creative choice, he tries out a new solution to this problem. At this stage of the argument, this new problem is a strictly personal one and the solution is employed because the agent expects that it will increase his utility. This novel response to a problem situation becomes an innovation when other individuals decide to imitate it. In other words, innovation is a social phenomenon because it relates to new problem solutions that are also viewed as new by other individuals. The reaction and imitation on the part of the other individuals gives rise to a cumulative process through which the new behavior or pattern of action becomes ever more widely adopted by those who expect therewith to better their condition. The diffusion of this innovative behavior among many or all members of a community brings about the solution to a problem that, from an external point of view, is a social one.

PABLO: I see, that is an invisible-hand explanation.[55]

STUDENT: Yes. A social pattern or institution arises, and the problem solving individuals do not have the overall pattern that is ultimately produced in mind, neither on the level of intentions nor even on the level of foresight or awareness.

PABLO: And you say that this mechanism is at work for all kinds of informal institutions?

STUDENT: Yes. I think that one should distinguish essentially between three broad types of institutions: conventions, moral rules, and social norms.

PABLO: Why that? Many theorists tend to speak generally about social norms which include all types of normative rules!

STUDENT: I know, but I don't think that this is fruitful. There is an essential difference between moral rules that are found in every human group and the immense variation of social norms which prescribe behavior regarding relatively minor issues.

PABLO: I see, you want to acknowledge the existence of moral universals.

STUDENT: I want to honor an important distinction, that's all.

PABLO: And what is the criterion of distinction among the different types of institutions?

STUDENT: The enforcement agency. An institution is not just a rule, but also the enforcement characteristics of it.

PABLO: I agree.

STUDENT: This is the reason that the same rule can be classified in different categories. The content of the rule can be the same, say "One should not kill"; and the enforcement agency can be of two kinds, say the individual conscience making it a moral rule and the state making it also a legal rule.

PABLO: So, what is the classification you suggest, tell me!

STUDENT: The conventions are self-policing; the moral rules are subsumed to first-party enforcement; and the social norms are enforced by the individuals of the group. These three types make up all informal institutions. Formal institutions are essentially the legal rules and they are enforced by the state.

PABLO: And you say that all informal institutions emerge in a process of a spontaneous interaction that no single individual can consciously control?

STUDENT: Exactly. The most important feature of conventions is their self-policing character. After they have emerged, nobody has an incentive to change rules that everybody else sticks to. In game theory conventions are usually analyzed with the help of what are known as "coordination games." Examples are traffic rules, industrial standards, forms of economic contracts, language, etc.[56]

PABLO: What about moral rules?

STUDENT: The moral rules are largely culturally independent, because they provide solutions to problems that are prevalent in every society, as Lawrence Kohlberg famously showed in his empirical research already in the 1980s.[57] The mechanisms for the enforcement of moral rules are entirely internal to the individual, and therefore no external enforcement agency for rule compliance is needed.

Typical examples of moral rules are "keep promises," "respect other people's property," "tell the truth," etc. These have a universal character. However, this does not necessarily mean that they are also followed, and in fact many individuals break them. In a sense, the empirical phenomenon to be explained is the existence of moral rules in a society, which are followed by part of the population.

PABLO: And according to your classification social norms are all the rest informal normative structures?

STUDENT: Yes. Social norms do not have a universal character, and they are enforced by an enforcement agency external to the agent, usually the other group members.[58] The mechanism of enforcement refers to the approval or disapproval of specific kinds of behavior. Social norms provide solutions to problems of less importance than moral rules and regulate settings appearing at specific times and places.

PABLO: And formal institutions are the outcome of the political process, so that they emerge deliberately.

STUDENT: Yes, this is a distinct mechanism, but the deliberate emergence of political institutions can be sufficiently illustrated if one employs the problem solving model. On a general line of argument and irrespective of the specific kind of institution, a social rule emerges deliberately whenever many individuals perceive the problem situation as a new one requiring a conscious choice. A shared mental model of the problem situation is formed after repeated acts of communication between the individuals involved in the collective setting have taken place. These shared mental models are the prerequisite of the collective choice that follows the communication process. The choice of rules is a conscious act of individuals mutually recognizing the existence of a social problem requiring solution. The final outcome of the collective choice depends on the configuration of interests prevailing at the time, and on how these interests are perceived and understood by the agents.

PABLO: It's all about power in the end.

STUDENT: Yes, in the end the collective decisions that lead to the creation of legal rules are the result of the political process during which individuals and organizations succeed to a greater or lesser degree in using the power that they have in order to impose rules that further their interests.

PABLO: But power, what is "power"?

STUDENT: I admit that what we call "political power" is very difficult to theoretically identify. But I think that the "availability of resources" is a good proxy for "political power"—the resources that players have is the decisive factor determining their behavior in the political game.

PABLO: But not only "economic resources"! I hope this is not what you want to say, because this would be a kind of economic determinism then!

STUDENT: No, there are three kinds of resources that are relevant: economic, political, and ideological. The degree of their availability to the players determines the extent of their bargaining power and thus how much they can influence the political process which in turn generates the formal institutions.

PABLO: I see. All that is, of course, pointing in the right direction, and one can indeed plausibly claim that formal institutions are the outcome of a deliberate collective choice and in this sense that they emerge deliberately and not spontaneously. In fact, many political scientists have defended a principal-agent theory in which the ruler deliberately creates formal institutions and public goods in exchange for taxes in a state. But all that presupposes something vital: that there is an entity called the "state" in the first place—that is, an organization with a comparative advantage in violence, extending over a geographic area whose boundaries are determined by its power to tax constituents. And I am not sure that the emergence of the organization that we call a state is itself a deliberate process.

Social Order and the State

STUDENT: I thoroughly agree. And here is a set of thoughts. A state exists because it provides individuals with solutions to the twin problems of trust and protection from aggression by individuals of the same society *and* those of different societies. A state emerges once a society grows bigger and relationships among the members become increasingly impersonal. In cases of larger groups or societies, trust becomes scarce since the discipline of reciprocity and the "shadow of the future" are relatively low. Individuals capable of learning are bound to realize that when they act within a large group, the probability of dealing with a defector increases. Since the content of individual learning depends decisively on environmental feedback, individuals acting in large groups must be expected to learn other lessons concerning the issue of trust than individuals acting in small groups. In other words, the content of the learning process of any individual living in a primitive tribe will differ considerably from the "lessons" acquired in a modern complex society. This differential learning process lies at the heart of the emergence of the state as an enforcing agency.

PABLO: So, the organization that we call the "state" is bound to arise once the society grows bigger and the relationships among its members become increasingly impersonal. But ... what do you think is the exact mechanism that leads to the emergence of the state in large societies?

STUDENT: This is a mechanism of spontaneous emergence, an invisible-hand mechanism. With the enlargement of society and its advancing impersonalization, it suffices if a creative individual realizes the potential benefit of cheating and starts to free ride on the promises given by the rest. If a sufficient number of other cheaters imitate him, then after some time an increasing group of free riders will be established. This, in turn, means that the environmental input of the other individuals, that is, the honest ones, will change. They will have collectively learnt that, first, cooperation is beneficial, but second that free riders exist in increasing numbers, and third, that the punishment or protection costs have increased because of the larger numbers and the subsequently increased complexity of the relationships.

PABLO: This collective lesson has the important implication, I guess, that a *demand for protection* will arise.

C. Mantzavinos, *A Dialogue on Institutions*, SpringerBriefs in Philosophy,
https://doi.org/10.1007/978-3-030-63016-4_3

STUDENT: Exactly, each individual will try to solve this practical problem by calling for violence against free riders.

PABLO: And then this demand must be satisfied, of course....

STUDENT: ...either by each individual separately devoting some of his time and energy to form coalitions against free riders each time they defect, or by a protective agency that will arise specializing in the provision of protection against free riders.

PABLO: But due to the immense transaction costs, mainly the costs of gathering and evaluating information on the exact nature of free riding, etc., a division-of-labour argument seems possible.

STUDENT: Yes, it is reasonable to hypothesize that some creative individuals will establish and run a business providing protection.

PABLO: But it is not reasonable to hypothesize that only one protective agency will emerge!

STUDENT: Of course not! A lot of such protective agencies, organizations specializing in the provision of protection by the use of violence in effect, will emerge.

PABLO: And they will trade protection against free riders for money or other goods!

STUDENT: Indeed. But protection can only be provided by violent means, which makes things complicated.

PABLO: "Protection" is a very peculiar service indeed! Availing of means of violence can, and in the vast majority of cases in fact does, turn "protection" to the "oppression" of the potential customers.

STUDENT: The only thing that restricts the entrepreneurs running those agencies are the informal rules of the game that are relevant for all members of the society in question. The mere limit to such oppression will be the conventions, moral rules, and social norms that these entrepreneurs bear, since they are themselves members of a cultural community. But as history teaches us these rules will hardly be sufficient to limit oppression!

PABLO: No, the limits that the informal rules impose on oppression will hardly suffice, but there will be a variety in the extent of the oppression by different agencies.

STUDENT: Yes, I agree. And these protective agencies will engage themselves in different kinds of relationships, cooperative or competitive.

PABLO: Yes, as I said before, managing violence is a complex issue.

STUDENT: But there is definitely a trial-and-error process involved here, too. I think you agree on that. Entrepreneurs will engage the protective agencies that they control in all possible relationships, ranging from armed battles to complete fusions of protective agencies in order to obtain better control over their clients. The outcome of this evolutionary process cannot be fully determined ex ante, since it depends on the creativity of the entrepreneurs, the rulers that is, their estimated chances to win the battles, and the effectiveness of their control over their clients.

PABLO: This process is really open; there is absolutely no necessity that it leads to the emergence of a single authority in a society that has the monopoly of violence. Political theorists that you seem to honor so much seem to systematically neglect this point![59]

STUDENT: I agree. The monopoly view of the state is only partially correct. It is surely fallacious if the alleged monopoly of force is meant to cover the whole society or cultural community—that is, all individuals with shared mental models and informal institutions. Think of historical counterexamples. They abound! The independent Greek city-states in antiquity[60] and the feuds in the Middle Ages are two good examples. There is no necessity, at least no economic necessity, leading to a unique organization controlling a territory. An economic argument could only be convincing if one could show that the provision of protection is an industry with the characteristics of a natural monopoly, that is with increasing returns to scale and a fairly inelastic demand, so that people continue to consume its products as the industry becomes increasingly concentrated. But I do not think that this is the case: Why should there be increasing returns to scale in the protection of life and property? Why must a large and concentrated state, that is, be more efficient in producing protection than many smaller organizations which in effect could be more responsive to the preferences of people?

PABLO: Like here in Colombia for example. Consider the case of the paramilitary leader, Jorge 40. One would misunderstand the phenomenon were one to think of him as a gangster or mafioso. In one-third to one-half of rural Colombia people like Jorge 40 are the state. Colombians called him "El Papa Tovar"—in Spanish, the Pope. In the San Angel plains of the Magdalena River in the department of Cesar, his "Vatican," he has ruled over his small empire of 20 armed fronts in three departments. His authority in that region of the Caribbean coast was such that peasants petitioned him as if he were a government official when land had been stolen by his men. A friend got access to a letter of a woman which was found by the police in Tovar's headquarters. It reads: "With my usual respect, I write to you to ask you to authorize whomever it corresponds to return my land in the municipality of San Angel to me [...]. I was evicted from this land four years ago and my family depends on it to survive. Today we wander from city to city looking for ways to make a living." Jorge 40 was not just a gangster; he was the state in Cesar.

STUDENT: This is amazing! And I have read that other groups were just as dominant in Colombia.[61]

PABLO: Yes. Ramón Isaza's "capital" was Puerto Triunfo in the far east of the department of Antioquia, where in 1977 he started his first paramilitary group, called "The Shotgunners." Isaza ruled the area for almost 30 years. One of his key commanders was his son-in-law, Luis Eduardo Zuluaga nicknamed "Mac-Gyver"—"McGuiver in Colombia"—after a US television character. McGuiver commanded the José Luis Zuluaga Front (FJLZ), which controlled a territory of some 5,000 square kilometers. The FJLZ had a written, of course very incomplete, legal system of "estatutos", statutes, that it enforced. It allowed rudimentary equality before the law in the sense that the same laws applied to members of the FJLZ as to civilians. The FJLZ also had a bureaucratized organization with functional specialization among the military wing, civilian "tax collectors," and a civilian "social team," which appears to have been remarkably unpatrimonial. The FJLZ regulated trade and social life. It had a mission statement, an ideology, a hymn, a prayer, and a radio station. It handed out medals, including the "Order of Francisco de Paula Santander" and the "Grand Cross of Gold." The FJLZ taxed every landowner and businessman in its territory. It even taxed drug dealers and cocaine laboratories, though it was not itself involved in the drug business (indeed, it rather disapproved of it). It built hundreds of kilometers of roads and extended electrification in rural areas. It built schools, and paid for teachers and musical instruments in others. It started a health clinic, rebuilt an old-age people's home, constructed houses for poor people, created an artisan center, and built a sports stadium and bull ring.

STUDENT: This is an amazing case indeed! And it shows convincingly that the monopoly of violence in a territory can in principle always be challenged for longer periods of time.

PABLO: People in the West seem to underestimate this. Having lived for decades in a "tamed" state, providing high quality public goods, they seem to forget that the core of the state lies in the management of violence and is very fragile.

STUDENT: Indeed. This is very important, what you are saying!

PABLO: So, the enforcing agency that we call a "state" does also emerge in a spontaneous process, and there is, thus, a certain continuum with the mechanism of emergence of informal institutions. But of course, once an organization specialized in the management of violence has been settled, that is, there is a "protective state" as James Buchanan used to call it, it also assumes productive functions and thus becomes a "productive state."[62] In modern times the productive state has grown hugely, to an unprecedented degree in human history.

STUDENT: I agree. And I would say that a "protective state" is characterized by a higher degree of stability vis-á-vis a "protective agency" since rulers and their coalition members and citizens have both gone through learning processes. Citizens have realized that the costs of exiting a protective state are quite high if exit is not explicitly allowed by the rulers[63]; and rulers have learnt how other rulers react and which technologies of oppression are most successful.[64] The difference is still one of degree rather than of kind, but there is a difference.

PABLO: To close the issue of state emergence, although it itself emerges spontaneously, once there, the rules that it creates are deliberately created according to the model of collective choice that you have outlined. The organizational rules of the state are the formal institutions of the society to the degree that this organization does successfully claim the monopoly of violence in a territory. Only in this sense is the monopoly view of the state correct—in the sense, that is, that the state creates and enforces rules for the specific group that it protects. As long as it is not challenged by any other organization, this group of people has no other alternative than to accept these rules. Do we agree on this?

STUDENT: We agree. The argument concerning the monopoly of force is correct only in the narrower sense that the protective agencies possess a monopoly among their own clients, that is, among the groups of individuals that they protect. In this simpler static sense, the state, once there, claims supremacy for its own authority and defends its claims against those of other persons and groups in the same society.[65]

PABLO: Now that we have reached an agreement on this, let me summarize: informal institutions are produced internally; that is, they are endogenous to a community. Formal institutions are imposed—in a way externally—onto the community as the exogenous product of the evolution of relationships among rulers or better organizations specializing in the management of violence offering protection to community members. The next step is to inquire into how "protective states" come to assume more and more functions, offering a bundle of public goods rather than merely protection.

STUDENT: And what do you suggest?

PABLO: We have to develop a general theory of how political markets work. Most theories apply mainly to developed polities like the United States, which operate within a network of fundamental constitutional and other political rules that remain the "unstable constants" in the short run.[66] A more general theory of politics would explore the transaction-cost characteristics of political markets and the role of ideology in shaping political outcomes.[67]

STUDENT: But is it appropriate to conceptualize politics as a market?

PABLO: But if the constitutive element of a market is an exchange process and the core of state activity is the provision of protection and other public goods to citizens in exchange for taxes, then politics is a market! It seems pretty clear!

STUDENT: I disagree. What you are suggesting is conceptualizing a great range of diverse social phenomena exclusively through a specific conceptual scheme, that is exchange. Nobody can negate that a variety of social relationships that unfold with respect to the control and use of violence in a territory involve some characteristics of an exchange process. However, much more is involved and the conceptual frame of a political market would not do justice to it.

PABLO: Why not? There is no conceptual scaffold which fits *all* dimensions of a complex social phenomenon, and the conceptual scaffold of a political market certainly does capture what we have agreed upon is the essential process constitutive of politics: the management and use of violence.

STUDENT: But the conceptual frame of "politics as exchange" does not capture appropriately the social processes that emerge when organizations and individuals endure, deal with, or administer violence. The underlying framework is one of representing the economic relation and the political relation through the lens of cooperation. Buchanan and Tullock have been extremely influential in presenting the market and the state as devices on equal standing through which cooperation is organized and made possible. People co-operate through the exchange of goods and services in the market in a setting which involves mutual gain—this is the "gains-from-trade" paradigm. The individual enters into an exchange relationship in which he furthers his own interest by providing some product or service which is of direct benefit to the other party of the transaction. After the exchange act, both parties of the exchange are better off than before. The same "gains-from-trade" paradigm is supposedly applicable to settings of collective or political action: two or more individuals find it mutually advantageous to join forces to accomplish certain common purposes: in a very real sense they "exchange" inputs in order to secure an output, which they can then share according to an agreement. They are equally better off after the transaction in comparison to the setting before the transaction. The familiar Crusoe-Friday story provides a nice illustration of this view. Crusoe is the better fisherman; Friday the better climber of coconut palms. They will find it mutually advantageous, therefore, to specialize and to enter into exchange. Similarly, both men will recognize the advantages to be secured from enemies by constructing a fortress. Yet one fortress is sufficient for the protection of both. Hence they will find it mutually advantageous to enter into a political "exchange" and devote resources to the construction of the common good.[68]

PABLO: Listen, Buchanan and Tullock had a normative intention: they wanted to provide a justification for democratic politics and they have devised a contractarian approach. What they wanted to show was in the good old tradition of social contract theory: we can all agree to some fundamental rules, to a constitution, if we all follow our own interests, and the hypothetical condition is that of a mutual agreement under a veil of ignorance. Because they were operating in the tradition of political economy, they tried to transfer analogically the "gains-from-trade" view from markets to politics. During this transfer process and stressing the possibility of conscious consent in politics, the fundamental issue of violence somehow disappeared. But this need not be so.

STUDENT: So you say that we can keep the "politics as exchange" view, unburdening it from all normative considerations, most importantly the social contract tradition in political philosophy?

PABLO: Yes. This is what I am saying.

STUDENT: Still, I am not convinced. The nature of violence seems to change everything—it imposes on us the adoption of a different kind of conceptual framework.

PABLO: Let me remind you of Mancur Olson's model of stationary banditry. Provided that rulers are taxing citizens in exchange for protection and they have a prima facie interest to maximize tax revenues, he shows that an invisible-hand process is at work even in the case of autocratic rulers. Even if rulers are not bound by any rules in their actions, it is in their own interest not to overtax their citizens and to provide some public goods, because only in this way can the subjects have the incentives to produce what then becomes the tax base. He claims that there is an invisible hand leading encompassing and stable interests with an unquestioned power to act, to a significant and surprising degree, in the interests of the entire society including those who are subject to their power. So the outcome of stationary banditry is not as bad as one would assume, and in fact even though most of human history is characterized by self-interested, extravagant rulers, the degree of economic progress is quite surprising.[69]

STUDENT: I recall Olson presenting these ideas in a lecture at the Center for the Study of Public Choice—this is the only time that I ever heard him speak. I was very young then, and it was the first time that I came in contact with the idea of stationary banditry lying behind the emergence of a state. I was impressed, because I had been socialized with a noble ideal of a state....

PABLO: .... as most people raised in the Western world are!

STUDENT: Though Olson's approach is much more convincing than the "gains-from-trade" view, in the end I think the "politics-as-exchange" paradigm hinges upon the term "protection" being left unspecified.

PABLO: Not at all! Provided that the whole process of state emergence takes place within a framework of pre-existing informal social rules as you have explained, "protection" means simply resolving conflict among constituents on the basis of existing informal rules. Self-interested ruling coalitions or organizations, even in autocratic systems will settle disputes among the constituents because this will provide an enhanced cooperation, and it will extend economic activities and thus the tax base on which they can increase their taxes, without a great cost[70]: setting dispute-settlement mechanisms is not very costly, and ruling coalitions will soon be able to learn this.

STUDENT: So, in the end, the state as an organization provides only for the enforcement of the preexisting social rules, the informal institutions. This is its core activity.

PABLO: But then as the ruling organization becomes bigger and more complex, a government that is, a set of formal rules will emerge, explicitly designed to direct government affairs and emanating from the conscious will easily identifiable in the person of the ruler or the collective choice of the members of the ruling organization.[71]

STUDENT: And this is the case of the deliberate emergence of formal institutions. Hayek clearly distinguishes between these two sets of rules, which are bound to exist in every impersonal society with a central enforcement agency; and he calls them law or "nomos" and legislation or "thesis." Legislation originates in the necessity of establishing governmental organization and appears historically later than law, which existed for ages before it occurred to man that he was able to make or alter it in a specific direction.[72] So, the big picture is this: the traditional "will of the legislator" was visible, at least in the first stadiums of human civilization, only in the rules pertaining to the organization of government, that is, in the commands of the ruler. With regard to the other group of rules, those regulating social behavior, no ruler had a long-term interest in affecting their *content*, but only in *enforcing* them.

PABLO: I have found Hayek's formulation of this issue unsurpassed: "A ruler sending a judge to preserve the peace will normally not do so for the purpose of preserving an order he has created, or to see whether his commands have been carried out, but to restore an order the character of which he may not even know."[73]

STUDENT: So, the fundamental insight is that in its beginnings the end of law, and its sole end, was to keep the peace.[74] And what I challenge is whether this whole complex process of management of violence and peace-keeping should be viewed through the conceptual lens of "politics as exchange."

PABLO: Be it as it may! What is most important is that the whole intricate set of formal and informal institutions "protect" the property rights of the individuals in a society—"property" to be understood, of course, in the broad sense which includes not only the material things under the command of an individual....

STUDENT: ...but also "his Life, Liberty and Estate, against the injuries and attempts of other Men" in the phrase of John Locke.[75]

PABLO: Not only legal rules, but also informal constraints define the rights of individuals drawing the boundaries of their protected domains within which they are free to follow their own aims. The property rights assigned to individuals in a society do not refer to person-thing relationships, as is sometimes assumed, but rather to person-person relationships. The property rights are best conceived, hence, as the "rights of action" of individuals within their protected domains.

STUDENT: And they can vary immensely, of course.

PABLO: They can vary immensely, yes.

STUDENT: In contemporary North Korea girls cannot ride bicycles; it's considered lascivious. All citizens must have government-provided portraits of Kim Il-sung and Kim Jong-il in their homes, and once a month, the police come by to inspect them. Children are raised to worship the late Kim Il-sung. There are 34,000 statues of Kim Il-sung in North Korea, and all wedding ceremonies must take place in front of one.

PABLO: So, there is a lot of choice within the "rights of action", choosing one of 34,000 statues in this case!

STUDENT: Indeed, there is a lot of choice! On the contrary, in the United States, citizens have the right to undergo a sex change operation for any reason whatsoever! They can express their indignation against the government and their country by burning their flag! And they are allowed to buy and sell stocks of companies as they please.

PABLO: The theoretical point of interest is that regardless of the content of property rights, or, to put it differently, the mix of formal and informal institutions prevailing at a moment of time in a society, a mutual stabilization of expectations takes place and social order emerges.

STUDENT: Exactly. In the case of informal institutions, the tendency of people to follow the same conventions, moral rules and social norms solves the problem of social order since the relative stability of their behavior makes it predictable for other agents, and in the end a global stabilization of expectations occurs, producing social coordination. It follows that when members encounter the legal system via formal institutions there is a learning process that each and every one is bound to go through.

PABLO: What kind of learning process do you mean and how does it unfold?

STUDENT: It unfolds exactly according to the mechanism that I have been talking about earlier: as a problem solving process of trial and error. The content of learning is very specific here. It is learning about the negative consequences of breaking the legal rules which is greatly facilitated by the fact that people are subject to a socialization process concerning informal rules from the very beginning of their lives. In other words, individuals are confronted with the normative dimension from childhood, and therefore it is easy for them to further adopt the legal norms in a later stage of their lives. Besides, a large number of legal rules are also acknowledged by the individuals as moral rules, social norms, or conventions, which further facilitates their internalization.

PABLO: I think that this is the critical point. As Ellickson has convincingly argued, ordinary people know little, if anything of the private substantive law which is applicable in their everyday lives.[76] They simply do not know the law and so they heavily rely on informal institutions instead. This is why informal institutions are more behaviorally relevant than legal rules.

STUDENT: I agree, people act primarily on the basis of only a scant knowledge of the *content* of legal rules. However, this does not affect their secure knowledge, though, that these legal rules will be effectively enforced. People use inferential strategies such as analogical reasoning and assume that, to a great extent, the moral and other informal rules that they have learnt to follow are also part of the legal order. Thus they adopt them more firmly because of the certainty that is provided by the existence of a central enforcing agency.

PABLO: I would not call it "certainty", however! In the vast majority, indeed in nearly all developing countries, this is not the case. The legal rules are simply not enforced by the state or to be precise they are enforced only eclectically!

STUDENT: Yes, of course, you are right. Citizens of different polities adopt the legal rules according to the environmental feedback they get in the course of encountering the legal system. If they have learned that deviation from legal rules is not always sanctioned successfully, as is the case in many Latin America countries, then their commitment to legal norms will be relatively weak. If the state as the enforcing mechanism of law sanctions deviations effectively, as is the case in Western societies, then the respect for legal norms by citizens will be relatively strong.

PABLO: Which brings us to the huge issue of the relationship between formal and informal institutions! As a matter of fact I think that this is a fundamental issue and we have to move on this frontier if we are to understand more deeply the emergence and working properties of the institutional framework of a society. Have you made any thoughts about this issue?

STUDENT: I think that abstract reflections on how formal and informal institutions interact will not lead us anywhere. One should rather specify the analysis of the relationship between formal and informal institutions with respect to a concrete phenomenon or outcome that is of interest. And the most important are two, I think. First, how do formal and informal rules interact to produce social order? Second, what institutional mix of formal and informal rules leads to a wealth-creating economic game?

PABLO: If we had an answer to these questions, we would have solved all political and economic problems of this world! To put it bluntly, we know a lot about polities, but not how to fix them. As someone who has provided policy advice for many years attempting to improve performance in countries like Colombia, I have been made actively aware of the shortcomings in our understanding of how to set them right!

STUDENT: I can imagine how important the relationship between formal and informal institutions is for policy reasons. Since policies consist of changes in formal institutions, but outcomes are a result of changes in both formal and informal rules and their enforcement characteristics, learning more about the interaction between formal and informal rules is a necessary condition for maintaining social order and improving economic performance.

PABLO: In an ergodic world we would eventually get it right, but in the world of continual change that we live in no such guarantee exists.[77] This is the first general point. The second is this: a mixture of formal institutions, informal institutions, and their enforcement characteristics defines institutional performance; and while the formal institutions may be altered by fiat, the informal institutions are not amenable to deliberate short-run change and the enforcement characteristics are only very imperfectly subject to deliberate control.[78]

STUDENT: And it is precisely this point that Acemoglu and Robinson seem to be missing in their otherwise interesting work *Why Nations Fail*.[79]

PABLO: I agree. But we want to move beyond them. Let us take stock now. Following methodological individualism you have proposed a problem solving model of individual behavior overcoming the old antithesis between *Homo oeconomicus* and *Homo sociologicus*. Rule-following when old problems come up and creative choice when novel problems emerge in the environment are the main essentials of this framework. In the process of communication that underlies social interaction, shared mental models are created which evolve over time. Informal institutions, that is conventions, moral rules and social norms emerge spontaneously. Formal institutions, that is legal rules are the outcome of political processes and emerge deliberately, although the enforcing agency of these institutions itself, that is the state, emerges also in a spontaneous process. Informal and formal institutions together constitute the rules of the game that structure human interaction. They enable the players of the game, individuals and organizations, to play the political-economic game because they are adopted by them and followed largely unconsciously. They are shared behavioral regularities directing the activities of the players, stabilizing their expectations and providing social order or disorder. They also channel market activities to a specific direction, thus enabling certain technologies to arise and a specific economic performance to result. And precisely this is something that we still have to discuss, because it is much more complex than it prima facie appears.

Institutions and Markets

STUDENT: But before coming to the relationship between institutions, markets and economic performance let me ask you something that has always puzzled me.

PABLO: I am listening.

STUDENT: What kind of statements are we entitled to formulate about institutional change?

PABLO: What do you mean?

STUDENT: I mean this: If one takes human creativity seriously, then an exact story of when changes in the institutional framework are to be expected and by whom they will be initiated cannot be told. Human creativity associated with an unconditional choice means that the future must remain open. Deterministic theories of institutional change are, thus, impossible. A full specification of the circumstances that will lead a player, be it an individual or an organization, to initiate a change in institutions is, thus, bound to fail. Do you agree?

PABLO: I agree.

STUDENT: But most economists did not seem to agree for decades, and they probably disagree even today. In most theories of institutional change, the suggestion was that institutions derive from the optimizing decisions of individuals and respond to changes in the set of relative prices that individuals face. Thus, when relative prices change, incentives are created to construct institutions that are more efficient. This was the narrative![80]

PABLO: There is on the contrary a persistence of inefficient institutions—Spain in the 17th century is just one nice illustration where the fiscal needs of rulers led to shortened time horizons and therefore a disparity between private incentives and social welfare.[81] The fiction of the existence of a benevolent, omniscient social maximizer. The typical disease of economists!

STUDENT: A further problem with that view is also that it implied the relatively quick and frequent change of institutions—due to the de facto frequent change in relative prices. But the very existence of institutions is explained, as we have been discussing earlier, by the need of individuals to have an orientation in a complex, uncertain world. They cannot change that easily and automatically after all.

C. Mantzavinos, *A Dialogue on Institutions*, SpringerBriefs in Philosophy,
https://doi.org/10.1007/978-3-030-63016-4_4

PABLO: No, they cannot.

STUDENT: The way I see it is that a change in institutions can take place in two ways. Either an institutional change is initiated by one individual and then imitated by others, so that an innovation is brought about and diffused in an evolutionary process, or an institutional change is initiated by many individuals acting collectively in order to respond to a new social problem. In both cases, the exact time and place of the institutional change obviously cannot be predicted. But even the less ambitious program of specifying the conditions that will facilitate institutional change cannot be pursued. The reason is that the solution to a personal problem perceived by an individual agent or to a social problem interpreted as new by many agents includes always a creative act, that is, it is fundamentally unpredictable.

PABLO: I like that. Go on.

STUDENT: An institutional change takes place whenever one or more agents think that his or their interests are better served under a new institutional arrangement than the prevailing one. This means that the agent or agents perceive subjectively at some point that their environmental situation constitutes a new problem. An external observer could predict that the specific environmental situation is bound to appear as a new one to the agents by pointing to the difference that exists in comparison to the past situations faced by the agents. For example, a technological innovation might change the distribution of income in a society, causing monetary losses for some individuals and monetary gains for some others. One could predict then that the problem situation in which one or more individuals find themselves, will be interpreted by them as a fundamentally new one. This prediction by an external observer can be met by comparing the economic situation of the agent at time t_0 to his situation at the time t_1 and by inferring that this change has been so dramatic that even the agent must have interpreted the problem situation as a new one. Once perceived as such, the new problem will be solved in a creative way. After an individual or collective choice, new solutions will be tried out by the agents, and these solutions will be outcomes of creative deliberations. These human choices, guided by interests as they are perceived at the moment, are not predictable, and therefore the institutional changes effected by those choices are not predictable either.

PABLO: I see your point, which is novel and important. And we can agree that the efficiency view of institutions is to be abandoned, since rulers will devise the property rights of the society according to their own interests and thus are typically inefficient. But on the other hand, I am not prepared to give up the task of predicting institutional change so easily. In fact, I am quite astonished that you seem to be willing to do this. I thought that the whole point of introducing shared mental models and thus belief systems in a systematic way in your discussion was exactly this: to highlight the role of "ideology" as an important factor which will help us predict institutional change. As a matter of fact this is my suggestion: to work out more carefully the theoretical link between ideology and institutional change.

STUDENT: But as soon as ideology is introduced into the analysis as an additional determining factor of institutional change, along with strictly economic factors, things get complicated. What is the exact role of ideology in affecting institutional permanence or change and how exactly is ideology linked with the prevailing economic constraints? When does ideology, when economic factors and when do both together contribute to an institutional change?

PABLO: Yes, these are the questions.

STUDENT: Well, I think that we can never answer them completely.

PABLO: Why are you so pessimistic?

STUDENT: Because of human creativity which dramatically reduces the possibility of predicting institutional change. Institutions may change in one direction or another according to how the agents choose each time and depending on what form the invisible hand process or the collective action takes. The future is open, and the direction of the institutional change cannot be forecast if the social process is to remain genuinely open.

PABLO: So, there is no possibility whatsoever to predict the content and direction of institutional change? This is a quite nihilistic result.

STUDENT: Here is my view of things. If you take an evolutionary stance, which I think one should take when one theorizes about institutional change, then one needs to identify one or more invariant restrictions[82] to which the social process should adapt in order for individuals to survive.

PABLO: Why is that, what do you mean?

STUDENT: In an evolutionary context you need a criterion of selection for institutions. Invariant restrictions would constitute such a criterion for selection since they would constitute at the same time the selective environment for a change in institutions. By identifying such invariant restrictions one could also predict the basic characteristics of the institutions that could exist in a global evolutionary process.

PABLO: What could such "invariant restrictions" be?

STUDENT: The functionalist view of society assumes that such a criterion could be the survival of the society as a whole. A global selection process of institutions could accordingly be modeled in the way that those "appropriate" institutions are selected whose existence contributes to the survival of the social system as a whole.

PABLO: But this does not seem to be consistent with your principle of methodological individualism, I gather!

STUDENT: Exactly. The only reasonable selection criterion for institutional evolution is the interests of the individuals in a society *as these individuals subjectively perceive them every time to be.* Hence, once an illusionary objective selection criterion disappears, only subjective interests, as the agents themselves understand them are left as a criterion of institutional selection. This individualization in turn, means that not even a vaguely constant or definite criterion for the selection of institutions exists and thus there is no possibility to predict the nature and quality of the institutions that will survive.

PABLO: This is a very pessimistic view!

STUDENT: I would say, this is a very modest view. But recall how dramatic institutional changes have been in history. Just think of the animal trials in the Middle

Ages.[83] Animal trials have been a normal institutional practice in the Middle Ages and even later. The attribution of responsibility to animals from the 14th to the 17th century was considered very plausible. Animals, including insects, faced the possibility of criminal charges for several centuries across many parts of Europe. The earliest record of an animal trial is the execution of a pig in 1266 at Fontenay-aux-Roses. Such trials remained part of several legal systems until the 17th century. Animal defendants appeared before both church and secular courts and the offences alleged against them ranged from murder to criminal damage. Human witnesses were often heard and in ecclesiastical courts they were routinely provided with lawyers. If convicted, it was usual for an animal such as a pig to be executed.

PABLO: Poor pigs!

STUDENT: What follows from this example?

PABLO: What follows?

STUDENT: That the only relatively secure theoretical proposition that can be formulated is that both ideologies and economic factors might motivate institutional change. But this amounts to saying that in fact everything can be a cause of change, since even if redistribution of income due to some technological innovation occurs, ideologies could neutralize the tendency toward institutional change and vice versa.

PABLO: I can see the point, I must admit.

STUDENT: Nobody can prevent, for example, a new prophet from appearing and propagating a new paradise on earth, one who will convince enough persons to follow him and to transform radically the institutional framework of the community. Such attempts at great transformations periodically appear in history — think of movements such as socialism or religious fundamentalism — and are not always due to the material or technological conditions prevailing within the respective society.

PABLO: And this has been Marx's error, of course.

STUDENT: Interestingly, Marxism resulted de facto in leading its very own predictions partly ad absurdum, in that it made clear the independent role ideas played in historical development.[84]

PABLO: Marx's theoretical centerpiece, historical materialism, rested on how material aspects of economic life together with technology shaped the "Überbau", that is all other aspects of social life, notably legal and political structures, but also art and science. So, this view acknowledges the role of institutions, but views them as derivative of economic fundamentals, of the powerful impulses unleashed by the forces of production.

STUDENT: To be fair, in some parts of his work he did allow for feedback from politics and other aspects of society to influence the forces of production, but economic determinism was certainly the theoretical centerpiece.

PABLO: It is probably not wise to indulge in Marxism now, but Marx was sensitive to all important issues: institutions, technology, ideology and markets. But he put all bits and pieces in the wrong order, he was too much influenced by bad philosophy and he had, of course, a political agenda.

STUDENT: I agree, we should not indulge in the subtleties of Marxism. But in order to clarify my own position, let me briefly refer to Marx and some other important political economists who have the ambition of discovering social laws of universal validity. This has traditionally appeared in two forms. The strong form alleged the existence of historical laws or laws of historical development. I think that Popper's arguments against Historicism had to do with this kind of a strong position and they are *grosso modo* still convincing.[85]

The weaker form concerns the somehow less ambitious quest of discovering the general laws of capitalism. David Ricardo predicted that a greater and greater share of national income would accrue to landowners and capital accumulation would terminate in economic stagnation. Marx followed with the general law of declining profits as capital accumulates and with the forecast of the inevitable immiseration of the proletariat. And recently Thomas Picketty pronounced the general law that "[w]hen the rate of return on capital significantly exceeds the growth rate of the economy, then it logically follows that inherited wealth grows faster than output and income"[86] and so a persistent inequality in favor of capital owners is bound to prevail. Marx's general laws of capitalism like those of Ricardo before him proved to be false. These laws were largely an extrapolation of facts and events of the time that the respective authors lived in into a supposedly general theory applicable at all times and places. When David Ricardo published his work *On the Principles of Political Economy and Taxation* in 1817,[87] and predicted a rising share of national income accruing to landowners, this was indeed the case in Britain where land returns were rising.[88] However, this trend was soon reversed and a monotonic decline of the share of national income accruing to land took place starting in the 1870's and lasting for the next 60 years. Marx's general laws, also failed, of course and Picketty's general laws do not fare better.

PABLO: It is because of the neglect of institutions. On this we agree!

STUDENT: Exactly. All these general laws systematically ignore the role of institutions that shape markets, prices and channel innovations. They are problematic for two reasons: an epistemological reason—they are founded on a pretense of knowledge—and an empirical reason—they claim that economic fundamentals are the primary cause for institutional evolution and change.

PABLO: This gets the causal order the wrong way, assuming that economics causes institutional change. They systematically neglect that it is institutions that shape markets, technology and factor prices and they falsely claim that it is the other way round.

STUDENT: Exactly. The main message of every institutionalist theory is that institutions matter and it is institutions that ultimately shape long-term economic performance. I agree, of course, with this position, however I find that it does have some weaknesses and is therefore vulnerable to criticism.

PABLO: But why is that?

STUDENT: Because we need an argument, a convincing theoretical argument, in defense of the right causal order from institutions to markets and economic performance, rather than the other way round.

PABLO: From a static point of view this is not problematic and is in fact the main insight of modern political economy: institutions come first and the analysis should be on what kind of impact existing institutions have upon economic activities of market participants.

STUDENT: But from an evolutionary perspective things are vastly more complex! Following the basic distinction between institutions as the rules of the game and activities within rules, there is an evolution both of the rules of the game and of the markets unfolding within these rules.

PABLO: Yes. And you have been arguing previously that there is no selection criterion for the evolution of institutions. This was your point. And you said that no prediction of an institutional change is possible.

STUDENT: Exactly. Given our current state of knowledge, the only possible explanation concerns *how* institutions have changed after their change has occurred. Only an ex post reconstruction of either a collective action or an invisible hand process that has led to the examined social pattern or institution is possible. In other words, the explanandum phenomenon must be an existing social institution and the explanatory hypothesis is the story of how it has emerged.

PABLO: You kept saying that human creativity is the reason.

STUDENT: To be sure, we cannot know whether the human creativity that underlies institutional change is itself determined or not. Logically at least, one cannot exclude the possibility that creativity is deterministic and that it is only our ignorance that forces us to treat it as nondeterministic. The reason a person happens to solve a new problem in one way rather than in another may depend on some factors that we cannot identify merely from the state of our current knowledge, but that we might be able to detect sometime in the future. The question of whether we will ever be able to explain creativity is, in any case, unanswerable.

PABLO: With respect to institutional evolution there is no stable selection criterion, no "invariant restrictions" to which institutions would adapt. This has to do with the role of creative choice in novel problem situations and immensely restricts the possibility of prediction; though an ex post explanation of institutional change is always possible. This is where we are now.

STUDENT: Yes. But my point is that with markets things are different—I am more optimistic there.

PABLO: Why?

STUDENT: Since both institutions and markets change, the function of social institutions as a selection environment for the evolutionary change taking place in markets is not self-evident, of course. Moreover, this proposition itself must be theoretically shown so that the whole theory can retain its validity, i.e. that the right causal order runs from institutions to markets and economic performance and not the other way round. In concrete terms, what must be shown is that the pace of change in institutions is slower than the pace of change in markets. Only in this case might institutions possess the relative invariant character with regard to market changes and allow for the formulation of satisfactory empirical propositions on economic evolution. Have you any better arguments?

PABLO: There has been an age-old debate between Alchian and Penrose in the 1950's on a similar issue on evolutionary theorizing in general, but this has not taken us very far.[89]

STUDENT: I didn't know that. The application of the cognitive approach to institutions that I propose provides a very strong theoretical argument in this direction in any case, I think.

PABLO: I am eager to hear.

STUDENT: When an individual starts exchanging in the market, she is already a socialized individual sharing the same social rules with the other market participants. She is not an ahistorical creature as it is assumed by standard neoclassical microeconomic theory. The important point is that agents possess knowledge concerning the rules of the game even before starting to play it. This knowledge is different from the knowledge she acquires during the market process because it is shared among all or almost all economic agents. During the socialization process, the individuals who later become the entrepreneurs of economic theory have learned the conventions, the moral rules and social norms of the society in which they are living. When they start their business, the entrepreneurs have learned which legal rules they have to respect and up to which point their private property rights are protected or violated by the state. They are already the "legal persons" of the legal theory. The entrepreneurs share the formal and informal institutions, and thus the rules of the economic game, by sharing the same learning history that makes them the specific agents of the specific economic game.

PABLO: I see. But why is the cognitive dimension important?

STUDENT: Let me employ the problem solving framework here. Since the mind is an instrument of classification that operates to solve the problems of the individual, whenever some problems have been tried out successfully in the environment for some time, the mind builds classes that prescribe the appropriate solutions to the respective problems. Every time the same problem appears, the appropriate solution will be applied automatically and unconsciously by the agent then. This is the case of old problems allowing for tested solutions stored in the repertoire of the mind and invoked automatically whenever needed. So, my claim is that when economic agents participate in markets, they have already classified all institutions as solutions to old problems in their minds. This is the internal, cognitive aspect of the prevailing institutions: the rules of the economic game have their counterpart in the available classes in the minds of economic agents and are, therefore, subjectively interpreted by them as solutions to old problems. What institutions effectively determine is the range of problem solving activities that economic agents do not need to consciously attend when participating in the market.

PABLO: And how does this subjective or cognitively internal counterpart of institutions, that is, old problem solutions shared by the economic agents explain why institutions change in a lower tempo than the markets?

STUDENT: Institutional evolution presupposes that problem solutions to social conflict are often tested by one innovative individual who is followed by others until eventually the problem solutions are *shared* by the population. Changes in institutions can take place only if all or almost all agents participate in those changes, either actively as initiators and imitators of novel problem solutions or passively by simply learning what the new solutions to the problem of social interaction consists of. A process of institutional change is completed only when *all* interacting individuals have formed the same classes in their minds…

PABLO: …the shared mental models.

STUDENT: Yes. Change in institutions is equivalent to the process of building shared mental models in the minds of all individuals. The notion of institutions as the rules of the game presupposes that *all* players have learned the rules before starting to play the game. This, in turn, means that changes in those rules are followed by a concomitant learning process of all players. However, since all players are involved in such a change, it is plausible to hypothesize that the tempo of the change in rules will be slower than that of a change in strictly individual behaviors.

PABLO: And I guess you want to say that this is exactly the case with the market process, during which economic agents are also learning!

STUDENT: Exactly. The main characteristic of the market process is that agents do not need to have shared knowledge. In fact, the contrary is true, since they are forced to acquire highly specialized knowledge. This is Adam Smith's main argument concerning the working of markets: division of labor induces specialization, promotes different skills and dexterities, and increases the productive potential of the economy. Division of labor goes hand in hand with division of knowledge among the market participants.

PABLO: Yes, we have learnt this from Adam Smith: the very essence of the market consists in the possession of different knowledge on the part of each market participant.

STUDENT: In order to survive under conditions of market competition, economic subjects are forced to specialize in different tasks and acquire different kinds of knowledge. This means that market participants run through different learning histories, because they are forced by market competition to confront *different* problems. The main characteristic of markets is the division of labor and, thus, the division of knowledge among economic agents, which is directly contrary to the case of institutions, which *presuppose shared knowledge of the agents*. Different agents face different problems. Then they try out new problem solutions to those different and usually quite specific problems and build in their minds, after some time, the respective classes of appropriate problem solutions to their own problems. This, in turn, means that knowledge creation, learning, and evolutionary change are faster in markets than in institutions. A process whereby everybody is experimenting with new solutions to his own problems, where there is no further need to share the knowledge that one acquires with *all* the rest, is bound to unfold at a greater tempo than a process that exists only insofar *everybody* possesses the same knowledge.

PABLO: Sounds plausible.

STUDENT: I am glad that you find it convincing! May I go on or is it getting boring?

PABLO: No, not at all. Go on!

STUDENT: Well, then here is what I was thinking about this issue. The shared knowledge seems to be the crucial factor that in the end channels the market process in a certain direction. Economic agents systematically avoid the behavior that is sanctioned by the institutions or systematically follow the behavior that is rewarded by them unconsciously. At the same time, they are freed from the need to decide anew about the most appropriate solution each time they face an old problem. By providing ready-made solutions to the agents, institutions, enforced with the aid of the sanction potential of the respective enforcing agencies, select at the same time which problems they do not need to care about consciously. Market participants are thus directed to solve certain categories of problems in the market context whose solution is not prescribed by the rules of the market game. This means that economic agents concentrate their innovative potential only on those problems that arise in the markets and are not dealt with by the institutions. These problems are subjectively interpreted by the economic agents as novel and allow for creative solutions that lead to monetary profits. In other words, in the market setting, agents learn individually by starting to solve new problems, testing solutions and building respective classes in accordance with their environmental feedback. In their learning enterprise, they do not need attend to the behavior of other agents concerning a large number of problems, as they can safely assume that the others will also have internalized the problem solutions defined by the institutions. The main effect of this coordination of expectations is the release of the learning potential of the economic agents, which can then be used when they participate in the market.

PABLO: And I guess the claim is that the main characteristic of problems emerging in the market is that they are temporary?

STUDENT: Exactly.

PABLO: It seems that the most important factor here is that the magical number in markets is "two". It takes only "two" to have an exchange transaction!

STUDENT: This is as simple as is true! Since for an exchange act to take place only two agents are needed, constant evaluation by market participants is possible and necessary. The diversity of exchange acts is immensely greater and more temporary than any recurrent social problem solved by social institutions. Accordingly, economic agents perceive in market settings a large number of problems as new ones, and therefore evaluate and consciously choose quite often.

PABLO: And choice takes place according to your own problem solving framework only when novel problems emerge, right?

STUDENT: Doesn't it make sense?

PABLO: It does, since it allows to accommodate both the traditional economic theory which deals exhaustively with choice in exchange settings, and the economic historian's insistence that institutions are the carriers of history and decisively structure those very exchange acts.

STUDENT: The fundamental asymmetry between institutional evolution and market evolution that I am stressing here helps also to illuminate the old debate concerning the roles of history and economic theory. History matters for the crystallization of the institutional structure. The role of history is to describe how the evolutionary process of institutions in a certain place and time occurred. The historical element embedded in the informal and formal institutions of a society, that is, conventions, moral rules, social norms and legal rules, aids decisively in *explaining* and *predicting* the direction and intensity of the competitive process within those given social rules. Historicity means nothing more than the learning history of the individual members of the society, which plays a crucial role in their economic behavior, and thus in producing aggregate economic outcomes.

PABLO: Yes, the controversy between economics and economic history has always puzzled me when they are two perfectly legitimate and complementary branches of research. Paradoxically, economics somehow won the political battle but lost the intellectual one, because by gaining independence, it became increasingly remote from economic realities, both past and present.[90] But tell me, how are we supposed to predict market outcomes in an evolutionary world, in a non-ergodic world? You kept saying that we cannot predict institutional change, but we can predict market change nevertheless? Is this the claim?

STUDENT: Yes, this is due to the fundamental asymmetry between institutional evolution and market evolution. "The market" as such does not exist. Markets are always embedded in a framework of formal and informal institutions. As long as this institutional framework remains relatively stable vis á vis markets through time—due to the cognitive reasons that I have mentioned before—it becomes increasingly possible to consider it as the selection environment of evolutionary market processes.

PABLO: So, you have found the "invariant restrictions" that you were looking for, though these are only "relatively invariant restrictions" in the end!

STUDENT: Yes, indeed. This is, I hope, a new idea on my part! Institutions as the normative rules of the game divide the range of possible actions of the economic agents into those that are and are not allowed. In the case of informal institutions the economic agents must fear social control, whenever they proceed with acts that are either not allowed or are disapproved by the society in which they live. The law on the other hand assigns property rights to economic agents, that is, the rights to engage in certain types of activities and the obligation to abstain from others in a more explicit form.

PABLO: And in the extreme case of a centrally planned economy, institutions are so extremely restrictive that no individual productive activities other than for personal consumption are allowed, of course!

STUDENT: Yes. The institutions determine effectively what range of economic activities is allowed to take place and under what competitive conditions. In a world of scarcity, we cannot live without competition. All we can choose is *what kind of competition* to live under—to the extent that we can choose it at all. As Demsetz nicely put it "the importance of the private property system is not in furthering or reducing rivalry generally but in the *direction* it gives rivalry. The harm to one individual in allowing competition may be as great as that resulting from theft, but we approve of the incentive effects of the former and disapprove of those of the latter".[91]

PABLO: This is very good! But let me tell you a story now!

STUDENT: A story? I am listening.

PABLO: Let me tell you a story that is recorded by the Roman authors Petronius[92] and Pliny the Elder.[93] There was once a craftsman who has managed to make an unbreakable glass bowl. He was given an audience with the emperor Tiberius in order to present his invention—with the expectation, of course, that he would receive a great reward. He tossed it on the pavement in front of Caesar Tiberius, but the bowl did not break. The craftsman picked the bowl up off the floor—it was dented like a bronze vase—pulled a hammer from his pocket, and smoothed it out very nicely. Tiberius asked then: "Does anyone else know how to make such unbreakable glass other than you?" The craftsman answered proudly that nobody else other than Jupiter knew the secret. Tiberius got alarmed that this invention would have as a consequence the devaluation of bronze, silver and gold. So, he immediately ordered that his workshop be destroyed and the craftsman be beheaded "lest gold be reduced to the value of mud!"

STUDENT: Wonderful story!

PABLO: What does this story teach us then?

STUDENT: What?

PABLO: It teaches us two things. The man has gone to Tiberius in order to get a reward for his invention, instead of setting up a business and selling the glass on the market to reap the profits. Secondly, Tiberius destroyed the innovation because of fear of the process of creative destruction, as Schumpeter called it[94] and the adverse economic effects which follow.

STUDENT: This is wonderful! It summarizes very nicely what I was trying to say.

PABLO: I am glad you liked it!

STUDENT: The institutions channel not only the direction of the competitive process, but also the knowledge generated during this process by defining which *action parameters* may be employed by the entrepreneurs in their problem solving activities. In markets, diverse entrepreneurs, with diverse capabilities and skills, struggle for profit and thereby create a dynamic competitive process. Under this competitive pressure, the entrepreneurs probe different problem solutions in the market environment that are intended to solve their primary problem, that is, the attainment of profits. The entrepreneurs by no means know how this primary problem can be solved.

PABLO: It is a non-ergodic world!

STUDENT: Indeed. Under conditions of genuine uncertainty their activities in the market are best conceptualized as an exploration of the alternative possibilities for making profits.

PABLO: Market activity as a trial-and-error process!

STUDENT: Yes. Entrepreneurial acts are hypotheses for finding a solution to the problems of economic agents, for example consumers, that is better than the other problem solutions offered currently in the market. Entrepreneurs perform tests in the market every time they offer a product of their hypothetical knowledge concerning the effectiveness of their action parameters in assuring them profits. In this profit-seeking enterprise, many action parameters are available to them.

PABLO: I would say a huge number: the localization of cheap resources, the location of the plant, the bribing of bureaucrats, the employment of skilled workers, the modes of financing production, the structure of the firm, the employment of different market methods, the design of different selling points, the quality of the product and so on.

STUDENT: My point is that the entrepreneur has only hypothetical, fallible knowledge concerning the effectiveness of every single action parameter and the effectiveness of the different mixes of the action parameters in making profits. Thus, every simple entrepreneurial act is undertaken in conditions of uncertainty and can best be understood as a hypothetical solution waiting for environmental feedback to come from the market. Entrepreneurial activity is indeed a trial-and-error activity, and competition is the process that arises from the rivalry of entrepreneurs when trying to test their hypotheses in the market environment in profitable ways.

PABLO: And your point is that only those entrepreneurial hypotheses emerge and evolve that are not disallowed by the institutional framework, right?

STUDENT: Yes. By allowing the employment of only limited action parameters by the economic agents, the institutions determine at the same time which type of knowledge will be tested and obtained by them. In this way, the institutions select which hypotheses will survive and which will disappear in the market process. At the same time they channel the innovative potential of the individuals in a certain direction.

PABLO: Let me mention a good example of what you are trying to say: piracy. If piracy is allowed by the institutions of a society, then private entrepreneurs will employ guns and knives as action parameters in their efforts to attain rents and will consequently acquire all the skills and knowledge necessary for their activities. To be a successful pirate one needs to know a great deal about naval warfare; the trade routes of commercial shipping; the armament, rigging, and crew size of the potential victims; and the market for booty. Successful pirates will acquire the requisite knowledge and skills. Such activities may well give rise to a thriving demand for improved naval warfare technology by both the pirates and the victims![95]

STUDENT: This is a nice, even if a quite extreme example! But let me proceed. The *dynamics* of the competitive process depend on the rate at which innovations occur and are adopted. This, in turn, depends on the payoffs, that is, on the utility increase expected from innovations and, thus, on the incentives to innovate. And these incentives crucially depend on the institutional framework.

PABLO: But still, in which sense can we predict market outcomes in this evolutionary setting, always in juxtaposition to the alleged (!) impossibility to predict institutional change that you kept repeating?

STUDENT: Here is the argument. It consists of two lines of thought: artificial selection and population thinking.

PABLO: I am listening!

STUDENT: The fact that it is institutions that act as the selective environment for market evolution implies a clear abandonment of any notion of natural selection in favor of the idea of artificial selection. With the term "artificial selection", the more or less conscious, purposeful selective act is designated in contrast to the term "natural selection". Inspired by animal breeders,[96] Darwin conceived of artificial selection as the conscious act of choice of the selective environment in order to achieve some desired results.[97] Now, by selecting the parameters of competition, institutions select at the same time, artificially, which entrepreneurial hypotheses will survive. The crucial factor is the existence of formal and informal institutions, which, being outcomes of human interaction themselves and partly of human design, impose a systematic influence on the market activities of the economic agents, thereby forcing them to adapt. The artificial character of this process consists in the fact that institutions are themselves human products.

PABLO: A somehow interesting analogy, though I am not entirely convinced why it should be useful. I hope the second line of thought is more substantial.

STUDENT: The second idea is that of "population thinking" advocated by the evolutionary biologist Ernst Mayr.[98] Population thinking is contrasted to "typological thinking" the main difference being the emphasis on the importance of the individual as opposed to the importance of the type. In typological thinking or "typological essentialism"[99] species are regarded as plausibly identifiable in terms of a few basic characteristics that are representative of their type or "essence". Based on mean values, one may, accordingly reconstruct the representative type of the species. In population thinking, species are instead described in terms of a distribution of characteristics, and it is the individual that counts. This stress upon the individual character of every member of a species implies the crucial importance of the variety in the evolutionary process, since it is on this variety that selection operates.

PABLO: This idea sounds more interesting. Typological thinking in the sense of Mayr seems to have gained a foothold in neoclassical economics: what else is the Marshallian "representative firm" of the industry,[100] that is the hypothetical firm with production costs that in long-run equilibrium are the average for the whole industry?

STUDENT: And here is how the combination of the ideas of artificial selection and population thinking yield the predictions of market outcomes in an evolutionary context, the context, that is, of genuine uncertainty. Let's start with a population in which all individuals differ in the traits or problem solutions that they employ, and this difference plays a crucial role in their relative success in securing rewards from the environment. This differential success is translated into different probabilities for the respective traits or problem solutions to be represented in future populations. It is predicted that only those traits or problem solutions will survive whose "individual carriers" are relatively more successful in adapting to their environment. Now this environment can either be naturally or artificially constructed. If it is an artificial environment, it can be predicted that the frequency of those traits or problem solutions will be higher in the population that help their carriers to be more adaptive to the artificial environment. Hence, artificial selection of individual traits or problem solutions has taken place. The notion of population thinking is important because it implies the continuous generation of variation within the population and the inducement of change in the distribution of traits or problem solutions in the population.

PABLO: And this, in turn, means that the artificial selection of traits or problem solutions does not impede the openness of the process. I think that this is important for an evolutionary account.

STUDENT: Exactly! The evolutionary process driven by constant variation remains radically open-ended due to the endogenously produced novelty. The artificial environment predetermines only the boundaries within which the whole evolutionary process can unfold; however, the adaptations to this environment are not themselves predefined. Artificial selection leads, therefore, to a regular and in a way directed change of the frequency of the traits or problem solutions created in the population, since the frequency of certain traits or problem solutions grows systematically, while that of certain other traits decreases.

PABLO: So, combining artificial selection and population thinking is supposed to express in a straightforward manner how market competition within institutions can best be understood in evolutionary terms, right?

STUDENT: Yes, from the population of problem solutions that are tried out in the market by the economic agents, those that help their employees to succeed in adapting to their institutional environment will occur most frequently. The systematic growth of the frequency of certain problem solutions due to the prevailing social institutions means at the same time that the knowledge of the economic agents grows in a certain direction.

PABLO: Which has profound implications for economic development and path dependence, I agree.

STUDENT: Yes, the view of the market that emerges from that is that it is an evolutionary process consisting of partial processes of arbitrage, innovation, and accumulation, which leads to outcomes in the form of prices, technologies, and economic development or stagnation.

PABLO: But it is, of course, coordination that has excited the interest of generations of social scientists.

STUDENT: Exactly. And this is how an institutionalist account of markets decisively differs from a standard neoclassical account. Schelling reminds us what an amazing phenomenon it is that somehow all of the activities seem to get coordinated in a market. "There's a taxi to get you to the airport. There's butter and cheese for lunch on the airplane. There are refineries to make the airplane fuel and trucks to transport it, cement for the runways, electricity for the escalators, and, most important of all, passengers who want to fly where the airplanes are going."[101]

PABLO: Amazement needn't be admiration, however, as Schelling equally reminds us. Once you understood the system, you might find ways to improve it considerably![102]

STUDENT: I agree. The proper understanding of the coordination issue will lead to completely different policy recommendations, this is true. In the standard neoclassical view of markets, this amazing coordination of activities takes place only via prices. Market participants need only perceive the price signals that will lead them to take the appropriate decisions in order for a market equilibrium, that is a result, to emerge. Whenever this does not emerge, there is a market failure, called in a crypto-normative vein "an inefficient outcome." On the institutionalist view, on the contrary, economic coordination is founded primarily on a "coordination of knowledge" rather than a "coordination of actions." And there are two layers of such coordination. First of all, the economic subjects avail themselves of shared mental models concerning the rules of the game. These take the form of shared solutions to old problems for the agents and provide a first basic level of coordination. The second level of coordination is spontaneously generated when the two sides of the market communicate during exchange. During the evolving market process, the evaluations of entrepreneurial hypotheses by the consumers implies the existence of an unintended price-making process.

PABLO: Yes. And we should be aware of the implications that this double layer of institutions and prices has for the issue of coordination.

STUDENT: Prices are certainly *unique* in expressing in an aggregate and measurable form the problem solution potential of the diverse entrepreneurial hypotheses. They represent aggregate statistics derived from free individual evaluations.

PABLO: However, the fact that prices are aggregate statistics does not imply that they are also *sufficient* statistics for the achievement of "efficient" resource allocation!

STUDENT: All that prices do, as extremely important as this is of course, is to reduce the amount of detail that the agents need to know in order to solve their problems.

PABLO: And let me remind you of something. What we have learnt after seventy years of experimenting with centrally planned economies is this: of course, the price signals lack all accuracy and precision relative to an external standard of perfection of an essentially nirvana approach. Although prices will often fail to correctly reflect scarcity, overall, more information is conveyed and utilized through a market price system than without one. A manufacturer might want to know the reasons for a change in the price of a specific resource in order to make better long-run decisions. But he is still better off with the price information than without it. Besides coordination, which is indeed an amazing phenomenon, markets and competition generate technologies as a spontaneous outcome.

STUDENT: Indeed.

PABLO: The organizations and entrepreneurs that participate in the economic game are primarily concerned with increasing their profits and technology is only one of the action parameters they employ in order to attain that. Insofar, scientific knowledge is used and technologically transformed by firms only to the degree that entrepreneurs expect economic profits from its use.

STUDENT: So, the generation of technology to a great degree must pass the market test and must stand profitability considerations.

PABLO: This is why the causal link between institutions, organizational activity, and the generation of technologies is not that straightforward.[103] This is the main point.

STUDENT: So, our conclusion is that economic performance is the outcome of a complex process of playing the economic game according to formal and informal rules that provide incentive structures and channel innovative activities in a certain direction.

PABLO: And there is no guarantee that the process of collective learning and the institutions of society that evolve over time will produce economic growth. In history the stories of failure are more frequent than the stories of success![104]

STUDENT: I think that we both agree that the complexity of this process of long-term economic development has been systematically ignored by standard neoclassical economic theory. The accumulation of physical and human capital and technological progress are nothing but secondary factors of economic development. The action is in institutions: the rules of the economic game define the incentives and more generally structure the behavior of economic agents, and thus channel their activities, lead to the accumulation of physical and human capital and technological progress, and in the end to economic growth and welfare.

PABLO: But what we need to know more about is what institutional mix of formal and informal institutions leads to a wealth-creating game! What we have very often is rather an unproductive game characterized by conflicts between groups for the distribution of wealth.

STUDENT: Certainly neither the formal nor the informal institutions alone are sufficient for economic development. The natural experiments that history has performed—probably the most credible kinds of experiments!—show this. Germany, China, and Korea were divided by the accidents of history and as a result came to live under different formal rules during most of the postwar period. The economic performance of West Germany, South Korea, Hong Kong, and Taiwan was incomparably greater than the respective performances of East Germany, North Korea, and Mainland China.[105] The informal rules that the populations in the divided nations shared did not reverse the different growth trajectories that they followed. Societies with the same cultural heritage but different formal rules will exhibit different patterns of economic growth.

PABLO: But societies that avail of the same formal institutions but whose populations follow different informal institutions are also bound to follow different economic paths. Formal institutions alone are not sufficient for economic development either. This is what we have learnt from the experience of a series of Latin American countries that adopted the U.S. Constitution in the 19th century but that did not achieve long-run economic development. And of course from the experience of the transformation process of the ex-communist countries in Eastern Europe. At the beginning there, the whole endeavour was "to get the prices right." The dogmatic transplantation of a set of formal institutions that prevailed for decades or centuries in the countries of the West to those countries of the East did not automatically result in good economic performance.[106] Formal rules remain a piece of paper if they are not followed by the citizens.

STUDENT: Yes, as long as formal rules are not "lived" by the agents, they cannot possibly yield any favorable economic effects. For example, the more than three hundred constitutional amendments that the Russian Congress of People's Deputies enacted between June 1990 and October 1992[107] presumably had no effect on the economic game other than to completely confuse the agents. Taking the learning process seriously explains why any form of "shock therapy" in the post-communist economies was bound to fail!

PABLO: It is only when an appropriately intricate framework of both formal and informal institutions is in place that long-term economic development can emerge. And we know only some bits and pieces about what works. Secure property rights are important, of course, as well as those economic institutions that secure open markets. This refers only to the content of the appropriate formal institutions, but there is of course the additional problem of the need for a credible commitment on the part of the state that these institutions will in fact be provided and enforced.[108]

STUDENT: And this is why it is so important that every society appropriately solve the problem of violence that we have been talking about[109]—not only in order to solve the problem of social order, but also in order to guarantee the functioning of a wealth-creating game.

PABLO: But at least with respect to the content of formal rules we know much more than with respect to the content of informal institutions. Here our ignorance is huge really. There are some hints and approaches like the classic Weberian *Protestant Ethic and the Spirit of Capitalism*,[110] which emphasizes the importance of civil society[111] and how an individualistic culture may provide incentives to capture the gains of trade more efficiently in the long-run,[112] but there is far more to learn on this. What is needed in any case is a high level of trust in a society, but this comes about as a reflection of a complex interaction in which beliefs and institutions are appropriately interweaved.[113]

STUDENT: Based on what we have been talking about, I think the primary conclusion is that it is rather rare that the spontaneous process of the emergence of informal institutions and the conscious design of a polity coincide in an institutional mix which is appropriate for a wealth-creating economic game. Two distinct processes of a different nature and following a thoroughly different direction must coincidentally result in a framework that facilitates economic growth. Looking at the world map, the chances that this will happen do not seem to be that high!

PABLO: And there is a second conclusion, having to do with path-dependence.

STUDENT: The recognition of path dependence is in fact the recognition that history plays a decisive role in the further process of institutional change, or, to put it differently, that tradition shapes the further evolution of institutions.

PABLO: Well, if path dependence indicated nothing more than the rather commonsensical position that the choices of the present are dependent on the choices of the past, then we could not claim that we have moved too far from commonsense!

STUDENT: There are philosophers who claim that science is nothing more than sophisticated systematization of common sense! So this is perhaps not that bad after all.

PABLO: But path-dependence is a much deeper phenomenon. Let me give you an example. Suppose that we are in front of an urn in which there are two balls, one white and the other red. If we put our hand into the urn without looking and randomly choose one ball, then the probability of the ball being white or red is 1/2. We proceed now according to the following rule: Each time that we choose a ball of a certain colour out of the urn, we put that ball into the urn, as well as a new ball of the same colour. If, in other words, we initially choose a white ball, the second time that we put our hand into the urn, there will be two white balls and one red ball. The probability of choosing a white ball will then be 2/3, whereas the probability of choosing a red one will be 1/3. If we again choose a white ball, then the next time, three out of four balls in the urn will be white. The probability that we will choose a white ball the next time will be 3/4 and so on. This is the Standard Polya Process.[114]

STUDENT: Very interesting!

PABLO: And it is a path dependent process. Each time that we choose a ball from the urn, the probability that we choose a ball of a specific colour depends on the colours of the balls that were chosen in the past and the structure towards which this process tends to settle. In the case at hand, the specific analogy between white and red balls depends on the path that has been followed. The events that took place at the beginning of the process are especially important since the overall number of balls is still small and the proportion of one colour decisively changes due to the addition of a ball of this colour. After time lapses, the overall number of balls increases and the perturbations have only a very minor effect: the structure that has emerged no longer changes!

STUDENT: Cannot we contend in an analogical manner that there is also cognitive path dependence?

PABLO: What do you have in mind?

STUDENT: The content of collective learning can be the same or similar over a number of points of time and so the mental models become relatively inflexible and shared belief systems are shaped. These are in turn the source of cognitive path dependence, since the more inflexible the mental models are, the more difficult their modification and revision become. And because of this cognitive path dependence, the "scaffolding" that humans erect on their environment, that is the formation of institutions, also takes place in a path-dependent way. Once all individuals have formed the same mental models, the institutional mix may start solving a variety of social problems in a particular way.

PABLO: One can speak of the "increasing returns of an institutional framework" in the sense that once the problem solutions are learned by agents, they are unconsciously applied each time similar problems arise. So, agents adapt to their social environment according to the prevailing institutional framework at decreasing individual costs. This can be called "adaptive efficiency."[115]

STUDENT: And it seems that this phenomenon exists because two mechanisms are at work. On the one hand, the institutions that have been created lead to the emergence of organizations whose survival depends on the perseverance of these institutions, and these organizations therefore invest resources in order to block any change that could endanger their survival. On the other hand, the second and probably most important mechanism is of a cognitive nature. Setting up institutions requires collective learning on the part of the individuals during which individuals perceive, process, and store the solutions to social problems in their memories. Since a considerable period of time lapses before this learning process is completed, the initial setup costs are very high. Once all or most individuals have internalized the rules of behavior, the institutional framework starts solving a variety of social problems in a specific way. Therefore one can indeed speak about the "increasing returns of the institutional framework."

PABLO: I agree. This institutional path dependence may structure the economic game in a standardized way through time and lead societies to play a game that results in undesirable consequences.

STUDENT: So, the combination of these two mechanisms leads along paths which a society cannot easily abandon, firstly because of the organized interests that resist doing so, and second because cognitive mechanisms make it easy or automatic to follow the rules of the status quo. We end up being locked into a path that frequently nobody or very few wished for, and nobody or very few have the incentive to start the enterprise of moving into a new path.

PABLO: So, is there any kind of conclusion?

STUDENT: The conclusion is that as soon as the institutional framework is relatively constant, market competition will be channeled into a certain direction and the generation of certain types of technologies will be encouraged. Thus, cognitive and institutional path dependence will ultimately lead to economic path dependence.[116]

PABLO: And very often, we end up being locked in paths that nobody really wished for.

STUDENT: A change from one path to another is, of course, possible. However, the process of the abandonment of one path does not itself include its telos. The new path does not exist somewhere out there, waiting to be discovered. On the contrary, every new path must be creatively constructed anew by modifying the existing rules of the game and by creating new ones. Whether the new path will be freer, more just, or more efficient than the old one remains unknown. Science just cannot deliver such a judgment. What remains is the consolation of political praxis.

PABLO: But let us take a physical path for now—that much we can do. We have to follow it to the Puerta del Reloj. Lili will wait for us there.

STUDENT: There she is. I can see her.

PABLO: Yes, and she is holding something. [...] Hello, my love. What do you have here?

LILI: This is a post card. Catherine sent it to us from Germany. It is from the Glyptothek in Munich. This is the statue of *Εἰρήνη*, Peace, who is carrying a child with her left arm, *Πλοῦτος*, Prosperity.

PABLO: Let me see [...].

STUDENT: The expressive means of Art are surely superior to those of both Science and Philosophy.

Notes

1. Robinson (2013, p. 43).
2. Robinson (2013, p. 43).
3. Weber (1992/1972, p. 29).
4. North et al. (2009, p. 259).
5. North (2005, Chap. 1).
6. Davidson (1991, p. 132).
7. North et al. (2009, p. 251).
8. Schumpeter (1908, Chap. VI).
9. Searle (1995, 2010).
10. Sen (1987, p. 12).
11. Newell and Simon (1972, p. 72).
12. See Holland et al. (1986, p. 10).
13. Ferguson (1767/1966, p. 6).
14. Smith (1776/1976, p. 362f.).
15. Popper (1972/1992, p. 261).
16. See Campbell (1974/1987).
17. Cosmides and Tooby (1992).
18. Gigerenzer (2000).
19. Pitt (2012).
20. Johnson-Laird (1983, 2006) and the list of the hundreds of articles on mental models at the website: http://www.mentalmodelsblog. wordpress.com.
21. Ryle (1949, p. 32).
22. Polanyi (1958, p. 62), Hayek (1967, p. 44).
23. Stanley and Williamson (2001), Stanley (2011, Chap. 7).
24. Ryle (1949, p. 30).
25. Ryle (1949, p. 31).
26. Hayek (1952).
27. Nisbett and Ross (1980).
28. Gigerenzer et al. (1999).
29. Gigerenzer et al. (2011).
30. Thagard (2005, Chap. 5).

C. Mantzavinos, *A Dialogue on Institutions*, SpringerBriefs in Philosophy,
https://doi.org/10.1007/978-3-030-63016-4

31. Fauconnier and Turner (2002).
32. Popper and Eccles (1977/1983, p. 126).
33. Campbell (1974/1987, p. 56).
34. Mantzavinos (2001, p. 41).
35. Shackle (1979, p. 54).
36. Shackle (1979, p. 2).
37. Holland et al. (1986, p. 11).
38. Knight (1921).
39. Darwin (1887/1969, pp. 232–233). For a discussion see Gigerenzer (2014, Chap. 8).
40. Duesenberry (1960, p. 233).
41. Becker (1976), Mäki (2009).
42. Goldberg (2001, p. 44).
43. Denzau and North (1994).
44. March (1999).
45. Anderson (1993, Chaps. 2–4) Cohen and Squire (1980).
46. Gigerenzer (2007, pp. 58ff.)
47. Hayek (1988, p. 68).
48. Hayek (1960, p. 26).
49. North (1990a, p. 3). See also Guala (2016, Chap. 1).
50. Gehlen (1961, p. 68; 1973, p. 97), Albert (1978, p. 24), DiMaggio (1997, p. 270f.).
51. Whitehead (1911, p. 61).
52. Hobbes (1651/1991, p. 89).
53. Hayek (1960, p. 66).
54. Ferguson (1767/1966, p. 188).
55. Ullmann-Margalit (1978), Nozick (1994).
56. Hume (1751/1975, p. 306), Schelling (1960, p. 91), Lewis (1969, p. 76), Young (1996, p. 107).
57. Kohlberg (1984).
58. Bicchieri (2006, 2016).
59. Elias (1939/1995).
60. Ober (2015).
61. Robinson (2013).
62. Buchanan (1975, pp. 68ff.).
63. Finer (1974, p. 80).
64. Nozick (1974).
65. Green (1990, p. 81f.).
66. Riker (1980). See also Alt and Crystal (1983).
67. North (1990b).
68. Buchanan and Tullock (1962, p. 19).
69. McGuire and Olson (1996).
70. Levi (1988, p. 43), Barzel (2000).
71. North (1981).
72. Hayek (1973/1982, p. 73).
73. Hayek (1973/1982, p. 98).

74. Pound (1959, p. 371).
75. Locke (1690/1991, p. 87).
76. Ellickson (1991, p. 144).
77. North (1994, 1996).
78. North (2005, p. 50). See also Picavet (2020, p. 143) and Ménard and Shirley (2018, part IV).
79. Acemoglu and Robinson (2012).
80. North and Thomas (1973).
81. North and Weingast (1989/1996).
82. Hesse (1987).
83. Evans (1906).
84. Albert (1976, p. 51).
85. Popper (1957, p. 41ff.).
86. Picketty (2014, p. 25f.).
87. Ricardo (1817/1951).
88. Acemoglu and Robinson (2015, p. 8).
89. Alchian (1950, 1953), Penrose (1952).
90. Bunge (1996, p. 5).
91. Demsetz (1989, p. 229f.).
92. Petronius (Satyricon, 51).
93. Pliny the Elder (1962, vol. X, Book 36.195).
94. Schumpeter (1942, Chap. 7).
95. North (1990a, p. 77).
96. Mayr (1982, p. 486).
97. Darwin (1875/1972, p. 3f.).
98. Mayr (1976, pp. 26–9; 1982, pp. 45–7 and 487f.; 1985a, p. 56; 1985b, pp. 76ff.)
99. Mayr (1982, p. 45).
100. Marshall (1920, p. 264f.).
101. Schelling (1978, p. 20).
102. Schelling (1978, p. 21).
103. Rosenberg (1994).
104. North (1998).
105. Olson (1996, p. 19).
106. North (2000).
107. Kiernan and Bell (1997, p. 118).
108. North (1993), Voigt (2020).
109. Weingast (1997).
110. Weber (1920/1934).
111. Putnam (1993).
112. Greif (2006).
113. Ostrom (1990, 2005).
114. Arthur et al. (1994, p. 36).
115. North (1996, p. 70).
116. David (1985).

Bibliography

Acemoglu, Daron, and James Robinson. 2012. *Why Nations Fail. The Origins of Power, Prosperity and Poverty*. London: Profile Books.

Acemoglu, Daron, and James Robinson. 2015. The Rise and Decline of General Laws of Capitalism. *Journal of Economic Perspectives* 29 (1): 3–28.

Albert, Hans. 1976. *Aufklärung und Steuerung*. Hamburg: Hoffmann und Campe Verlag.

Albert, Hans. 1978. *Traktat über Rationale Praxis*. Tübingen: J.C.B. Mohr (Paul Siebeck).

Alchian, Armen. 1950. Uncertainty, Evolution and Economic Theory. *Journal of Political Economy* 58: 211–221.

Alchian, Armen. 1953. Comment. *American Economic Review* 43: 600–603.

Alt, James, and Alec, Chrystal. 1983. *Political Economics*. Berkeley: University of California Press.

Anderson, John R. 1993. *Rules of Mind*. Hillsdale, NJ: Lawrence Erlbaum Associates.

Arthur, Brian, Y.M. Ermoliev, and Y.M. Kaniovskik. 1994. Path-Dependent Processes and the Emergence of Micro-Structure. In *Increasing Returns and Path Dependence in the Economy*, ed. Brian Arthur, 33–48. Ann Arbor: University of Michigan Press.

Barzel, Yoram. 2000. Property Rights and the Evolution of the State. *Economics of Governance* 1: 25–51.

Becker, Gary. 1976. *The Economic Approach to Human Behavior*. Chicago: The University of Chicago Press.

Bicchieri, Cristina. 2006. *The Grammar of Society. The Nature and Dynamics of Social Norms*. Cambridge: Cambridge University Press.

Bicchieri, Cristina. 2016. *Norms in the Wild: How to Diagnose, Measure and Change Social Norms*. Oxford: Oxford University Press.

Buchanan, James. 1975. *The Limits of Liberty. Between Anarchy and Leviathan*. Chicago: The University of Chicago Press.

Buchanan, James M., and Tullock Gordon. 1962. *The Calculus of Consent. Logical Foundations of Constitutional Democracy*. Ann Arbor: The University of Michigan Press.

Bunge, Mario. 1996. *Finding Philosophy in Social Science*. New Haven and London: Yale University Press.

Campbell, Donald T. 1974/1987. Evolutionary Epistemology, originally published in *The Philosophy of Karl Popper*, ed. Paul A. Schlipp, 413–463. La Salle, Ill.: Open Court, 1974 and reprinted in: *Evolutionary Epistemology, Rationality and the Sociology of Knowledge*, ed. Gerard Radnitszky and W.W. Bartley III, 48–114. La Salle, Ill.: Open Court, 1987.

Cohen, Neal J., and Larry R. Squire. 1980. Preserved Learning and Retention of Pattern-Analyzing Skill in Amnesia: Dissociation of Knowing How and Knowing That. *Science* 210: 207–210.

Cosmides, Leda, and Tooby John. 1992. *The Adapted Mind. Evolutionary Psychology and the Generation of Culture*. New York: Oxford University Press.

David, Paul. 1985. Clio and the Economics of QWERTY. *American Economic Review* 75: 382–387.

C. Mantzavinos, *A Dialogue on Institutions*, SpringerBriefs in Philosophy,
https://doi.org/10.1007/978-3-030-63016-4

Davidson, Paul. 1991. Is Probability Theory Relevant for Uncertainty? A Post-Keynesian Perspective. *Journal of Economic Perspectives* 5 (1): 129–143.
Darwin, Charles. 1875/1972. *The Variation of Animals and Plants Under Domestication*, 2nd ed. New York: AMS Press.
Darwin, Charles. 1887/1969. *The Autobiography of Charles Darwin, 1809–1882*, ed. N. Barlow. New York: Norton.
Demsetz, Harold. 1989. *Efficiency, Competition and Policy. The Organization of Economic Activity*, vol. II. Oxford: Basil Blackwell.
Denzau, Arthur, and Douglass C. North. 1994. Shared Mental Models. Ideologies and Institutions. *Kyklos* 47: 3–31.
DiMaggio, Paul. 1997. Culture and Cognition. *Annual Review of Sociology* 23: 263–287.
Duesenberry, James. 1960. An Economic Analysis of Fertility: Comment. In *Demographic and Economic Change in Developed Countries*, 231–234. Princeton: Princeton University Press.
Elias, Norbert. 1939/1995. *Über den Prozeß der Zivilisation*, vol. 2, 19th ed. Frankfurt am Main: Suhrkamp.
Ellickson, Robert. 1991. *Order Without Law*. Cambridge, MA: Harvard University Press.
Evans, E.P. 1906. *The Criminal Prosecution and Capital Punishment of Animals*. New York: E. P. Dutton and Company.
Fauconnier, Gilles, and Mark Turner. 2002. *The Way We Think: Conceptual Blending and the Mind's Hidden Complexities*. New York: Basic Books.
Ferguson, Adam. 1767/1966. *An Essay on the History of Civil Society*. Edinburgh: Edinburgh University Press.
Finer, Samuel E. 1974. State-Building, State Boundaries and Border Control. *Social Science Information* 13: 79–126.
Gehlen, Arnold. 1961. *Anthropologische Forschung*. Reinbeck bei Hamburg: Rowohlt.
Gehlen, Arnold. 1973. *Moral und Hypermoral – Eine pluralistische Ethik*. Frankfurt a.M.: Athenäum Verlag.
Gigerenzer, Gerd. 2000. *Adaptive Thinking: Rationality in the Real World*. Oxford: Oxford University Press.
Gigerenzer, Gerd. 2007. *Gut Feelings. The Intelligence of the Unconscious*. London: Penguin Books.
Gigerenzer, Gerd. 2014. *Risk Savvy. How to Make Good Decisions*. London and New York: Viking.
Gigerenzer, Gerd, Peter M. Todd, and the ABC Research Group. 1999. *Simple Heuristics that Make Us Smart*. Oxford: Oxford University Press.
Gigerenzer, Gerd, Ralph Hertwig, and Thorsten Pachur (eds.). 2011. *Heuristics: The Foundations of Adaptive Behavior*. Oxford: Oxford University Press.
Goldberg, Elkohon. 2001. *The Executive Brain: Frontal Lobes and the Civilized Mind*. Oxford: Oxford University Press.
Green, Leslie. 1990. *The Authority of the State*. Oxford: Clarendon Press.
Greif, Avner. 2006. *Institutions and the Path to Modern Economy: Lessons from Medieval Trade*. Cambridge: Cambridge University Press.
Guala, Francesco. 2016. *Understanding Institutions. The Science and Philosophy of Living Together*. Princeton, NJ. Princeton University Press.
Hayek, Friedrich A. von. 1952. *The Sensory Order. An Inquiry into the Foundations of Theoretical Psychology*. London: Routledge & Kegan Paul.
Hayek, Friedrich A. von. 1960. *The Constitution of Liberty*. London: Routledge & Kegan Paul.
Hayek, Friedrich A. von. 1967. *Studies in Philosophy, Politics and Economics*. London: Routledge & Kegan Paul.
Hayek, Friedrich A. von. 1973/1982. *Rules and Order, vol. I of Law, Legislation and Liberty*. London: Routledge & Kegan Paul.
Hayek, Friedrich A. von. 1988. *The Fatal Conceit: The Errors of Socialism*. Chicago: The University of Chicago Press.

Hesse, Günter. 1987. Innovationen und Restriktionen. Zum Ansatz der Theorie der langfristigen Entwicklung. In *Markt und Wettbewerb. Festschrift für Ernst Heuß zum 65. Geburtstag*, ed. Manfred Borchert, Ulrich Fehl and Peter Oberender, 195–226. Bern und Stuttgart: Paul Haupt.
Hobbes, Thomas. 1651/1991. *Leviathan*, ed. Richard Tuck. Cambridge: Cambridge University Press.
Holland, John H., Keith J. Holyoak, Richard Nisbett, and Paul Thagard. 1986. *Induction: Processes of Inference, Learning and Discovery*. Cambridge/MA: The MIT Press.
Hume, David. 1751/1975. *An Enquiry Concerning the Principles of Morals*. Oxford: Oxford University Press.
Johnson-Laird, Philip N. 1983. *Mental Models*. Cambridge, MA: Harvard University Press.
Johnson-Laird, Philip N. 2006. *How We Reason*. Oxford: Oxford University Press.
Kiernan, Brenan, and Francis X. Bell. 1997. Legislative Politics and the Political Economy of Property Rights in Post-Communist Russia. In *The Political Economy of Property Rights*, ed. David L. Weimer. Cambridge: Cambridge University Press.
Knight, Frank H. 1921. *Risk, Uncertainty and Profit*. Chicago: The University of Chicago Press.
Kohlberg, Lawrence. 1984. *Essays in Moral Development, Vol. II: The Psychology of Moral Development. The Nature and Validity of Moral Stages*. New York: Harper & Row.
Levi, Margaret. 1988. *Of Rule and Revenue*. Berkeley: University of California Press.
Lewis, David. 1969. *Convention. A Philosophical Study*. Oxford: Basil Blackwell.
Locke, John. 1690/1991. *Two Treatises of Government*, 2nd ed., ed. Peter Laslett. Cambridge: Cambridge University Press.
Mäki, Uskali. 2009. Economics Imperialism: Concepts and Constraints. *Philosophy of the Social Sciences* 39: 351–380.
Mantzavinos, C. 1994. *Wettbewerbstheorie*. Berlin: Duncker & Humblot.
Mantzavinos, C. 2001. *Individuals, Institutions, and Markets*. Cambridge: Cambridge University Press.
Mantzavinos, C., Douglass C. North, and Syed Shariq. 2004. Learning, Institutions, and Economic Performance. *Perspectives on Politics* 2: 75–84.
March, James G. 1999. *The Pursuit of Organizational Intelligence*. Oxford: Blackwell Press.
Marshall, Alfred. 1920. *Principles of Economics*, 8th ed. London: Macmillan Press.
Mayr, Ernst. 1976. *Evolution and the Diversity of Life: Selected Essays*. Cambridge/MA: Harvard University Press.
Mayr, Ernst. 1982. *The Growth of Biological Thought*. Cambridge/MA: Harvard University Press.
Mayr, Ernst. 1985. How Biology Differs from the Physical Sciences. In *Evolution at the Crossroads: The New Biology and the New Philosophy of Science*, ed. David J. Depew and Bruce H. Weber, 43-63. Cambridge/MA: The MIT Press.
Mayr, Ernst. 1985. Darwin's Five Theories of Evolution. In *The Darwinian Heritage*, ed. David Kohn, 755–772. Princeton University Press.
McGuire, Martin C., and Mancur Olson. 1996. The Economics of Autocracy and Majority Rule: The Invisible Hand and the Use of Force. *Journal of Economic Literature* 34: 72–96.
Ménard, Claude, and Mary Shirley (eds.). 2018. *A Research Agenda for New Institutional Economics*. Cheltenham and Northampton: Edward Elgar.
Newell, Allan, and Simon Herbert. 1972. *Human Problem Solving*. Englewood Cliffs, NJ: Prentice-Hall.
Nisbett, Richard, and Lee Ross. 1980. *Human Inference: Strategies and Shortcomings of Social Judgment*. Englewood Cliffs, NJ: Prentice-Hall.
North, Douglass C. 1981. *Structure and Change in Economic History*. New York: W.W. Norton.
North, Douglass C. 1990a. *Institutions, Institutional Change and Economic Performance*. Cambridge: Cambridge University Press.
North, Douglass C. 1990b. A Transaction-Cost Theory of Politics. *Journal of Theoretical Politics* 2 (4): 355–367.
North, Douglass C. 1993. Institutions and Credible Commitments. *Journal of Institutional and Theoretical Economics* 149: 11–23.

North, Douglass C. 1994. Economic Performance Through Time. *American Economic Review* 84: 359–368.

North, Douglass C. 1996. Economic Performance Through Time: The Limits to Knowledge. Unpublished paper presented at the Conference on Fundamental Limits to Knowledge in Economics at the Santa Fe Institute, Santa Fe, New Mexico, July 31–August 3.

North, Douglass C. 1998. Where Have We Been and Where Are We Going? In *Economics, Values, and Organization*, ed. Avner Ben-Ner and Louis Putterman, 491–508. Cambridge: Cambridge University Press.

North, Douglass C. 2000. Big-Bang Transformations of Economic Systems: An Introductory Note. *Journal of Institutional and Theoretical Economics* 156: 3–8.

North, Douglass C. 2005. *Understanding the Process of Economic Change*. Princeton, NJ: Princeton University Press.

North, Douglass C., and Thomas Robert. 1973. *The Rise of the Western World: A New Economic History*. Cambridge: Cambridge University Press.

North, Douglass C., and Barry R. Weingast. 1989/1996. Constitutions and Commitment: The Evolution of Institutions Governing Public Choice in Seventeenth-Century England. *The Journal of Economic History* 149, 803–832 and reprinted in: Lee J. Alson, Thráinn Eggertsson and Douglass C. North (eds.): Empirical Studies in Institutional Change, Cambridge: Cambridge University Press, pp. 134–165.

North, Douglass C., John Wallis, and Barry Weingast. 2009. *Violence and Social Orders*. Cambridge: Cambridge University Press.

Nozick, Robert. 1974. *Anarchy, State and Utopia*. Oxford: Blackwell.

Nozick, Robert. 1994. Invisible-Hand Explanations. *American Economic Review (Papers and Proceedings)* 84: 314–318.

Ober, Josiah. 2015. *The Rise and Fall of Classical Greece*. Princeton, NJ: Princeton University Press.

Olson, Mancur. 1996. Big Bills Left on the Sidewalk: Why Some Nations Are Rich and Other Poor. *Journal of Economic Perspectives* 10: 3–24.

Ostrom, Elinor. 1990. *Govering the Commons. The Evolution of Institutions for Collective Action*. Cambridge: Cambridge University Press.

Ostrom, Elinor. 2005. *Understanding Institutional Diversity*. Princeton: Princeton University Press.

Penrose, Edith. 1952. Biological Analogies in the Theory of the Firm. *American Economic Review* 42: 804–819.

Petronius. 1996. *Satyrica*, transl. by R. Bracht Branham and Daniel Kinney. Los Angeles: University of California Press.

Picavet, Emmanuel. 2020. Ways of Compromise-Building in a World of Institutions. In *Institutions in Action. The Nature and Role of Institutions in the Real World*, eds. Andina, Tiziana and Petar Bojanic, 135–145. Heidelberg and New York: Springer.

Picketty, Thomas. 2014. *Capital in the Twenty-First Century*. Cambridge, MA: Harvard University Press.

Pitt, David. 2012. Mental Representation. In *The Stanford Encyclopedia of Philosophy*. plato.stanford.edu/entries/mental-representation.

Pliny the Elder. 1962. *Natural History*, vol. X, Books 36–37, Loeb Classical Library. Cambridge/MA: Harvard University Press.

Polanyi, Michael. 1958. *Personal Knowledge*. London: Routledge.

Popper, Karl. 1957. *The Poverty of Historicism*. London: Routledge.

Popper, Karl. 1972/1992. *Objective Knowledge. An Evolutionary Approach*. Oxford: Clarendon Press.

Popper, Karl, and John Eccles. 1977/1983. *The Self and its Brain. An Argument for Interactionism*. London: Routledge.

Pound, Roscoe. 1959. *Jurisprudence*, vol. I. New York: Foundation Press.

Putnam, Robert. 1993. *Making Democracy Work*. Princeton, NJ: Princeton University Press.

Ricardo, David. 1817/1951. *On the Principles of Political Economy and Taxation*, ed. Pierro Sraffa. Cambridge: Cambridge University Press.

Riker, William. 1980. Implications from the Disequilibrium of Majority Rule for the Study of Institutions. *American Political Science Review* 74: 432–446.

Robinson, James. 2013. Colombia: Another 100 Years of Solitude? In *Current History*, vol. 112 (751), February 2013, 43–48.

Rosenberg, Nathan. 1994. *Exploring the Black Box: Technology, Economics, and History.* Cambridge: Cambridge University Press.

Ryle, Gilbert. 1949. *The Concept of Mind.* London: Penguin Books.

Searle, John. 1995. *The Construction of Social Reality.* New York: The Free Press.

Searle, John. 2010. *Making the Social World: The Structure of Human Civilization.* Oxford: Oxford University Press.

Schelling, Thomas C. 1960. *The Strategy of Conflict.* Cambridge, MA: Harvard University Press.

Schelling, Thomas C. 1978. *Micromotives and Macrobehavior.* New York and London: W.W. Norton & Company.

Schumpeter, Joseph Alois. 1908. *Das Wesen und der Hauptinhalt der theoretischen Nationalökonomie.* Berlin: Duncker & Humblot.

Schumpeter, Joseph Alois. 1942. *Capitalism, Socialism, and Democracy.* New York: Harper & Row Publishers.

Sen, Amartya. 1987. *On Ethics and Economics.* Oxford and Cambridge, MA: Blackwell.

Shackle, G.L.S. 1979. *Imagination and the Nature of Choice.* Edinburgh: Edinburgh University Press.

Smith, Adam. 1776/1976. *An Inquiry into the Nature and Causes of the Wealth of Nations*, ed. Edwin Cannan. Chicago: The University of Chicago Press.

Stanley, Jason. 2011. *Know How.* Oxford: Oxford University Press.

Stanley, Jason, and Timothy Williamson. 2001. Knowing How. *The Journal of Philosophy* 98: 411–444.

Thagard, Paul. 2005. *Mind: Introduction to Cognitive Science*, 2nd ed. Cambridge/MA: The MIT Press.

Ullmann-Margalit, Edna. 1978. Invisible-Hand Explanations. *Synthese* 39: 263–291.

Voigt, Stefan. 2020. Mind the Gap – Analyzing the Divergence between Constitutional Text and Constitutional Reality, *ILE Working Paper Series, No. 32, University of Hamburg, Institute of Law and Economics (ILE), Hamburg*

Weber, Max. 1920/1934. *Die Protestantische Ethik und der Geist des Kapitalismus.* J.C.B. Mohr (Paul Siebeck).

Weber, Max. 1922/1972. *Wirtschaft und Gesellschaft*, 5th ed. Tübingen: J.C.B. Mohr (Paul Siebeck).

Weingast, Barry. 1997. The Political Foundations of Democracy and the Rule of Law. *American Political Science Review* 91: 245–263.

Whitehead, Alfred N. 1911. *Introduction to Mathematics.* London: Williams and Norgate.

Young, H. Peyton. 1996. The Economics of Convention. *Journal of Economic Perspectives* 10: 105–122.